PATTERNS
FOR CANVAS
EMBROIDERY

PATTERNS FOR CANVAS EMBROIDERY

Diana Jones

BT Batsford Ltd
London

ISBN 0 7134 3285 3

Filmset in 11/12pt 'Monophoto' Univers light by
Servis Filmsetting Ltd, Manchester
Printed by The Anchor Press Ltd, Tiptree, Essex
for the publishers BT Batsford Ltd
4 Fitzhardinge Street, London W1H 0AH

Contents

Acknowledgment

Roger Warren for the photographs.
Kate Banister for working the design in
the squab cushion shown in colour.
and Rachel Jones for designing and
working the pattern of the jacket.

Introduction

To suppose that every needlewoman can be her own designer is perhaps wishful thinking. Most of us need guidance. There is so much to learn from the past, in design, in technical accomplishment, but most of all in the fact that it used to be considered necessary to provide the untrained designer with well devised and well constructed patterns. It can be left to the individual to modify, amend or develop, given a flexible framework. The aim of this book is an attempt to provide that framework.

It is intended for all levels of skill starting with beginners or children and yet including more elaborate examples for the most proficient. Many of these patterns are traditional in origin but like any product of a strong tradition their capacity for modification keeps them alive and interesting.

Embroidery is a labour of love. If there is no pleasure in the making, it is not worth the doing. This is not to say that the time cannot be spent making things that are not only beautiful but useful too. Of all the many and various forms of embroidery canvas work is probably the most practical. The problem of having to produce a strong, hard-wearing fabric can be a welcome discipline keeping the embroideress from impractical flights of fancy. More than a limiting factor it

becomes a contributing one. It provides another dimension: the feel of the embroidery becomes as important as the look of it; each is dependent on the other. Different textures produced by contrast of stitching and closely worked surfaces invite the hand to feel them. Only canvas work can produce such richness of texture combined with a flexibility of design.

To call canvas embroidery 'tapestry' is to confuse the structure of both textiles. True tapestry is woven on a loom, a woollen weft on linen or woollen warp. In the past it was used for large hangings to decorate and insulate walls. Canvas embroidery means stitching with a needle over an openweave of linen or cotton with woollen and sometimes silk threads. The stitching is more than simply decoration, it alters the basic fabric converting it to a warm, thick, hard-wearing surface. It has been used for upholstery, bags, cushions, etc., since the sixteenth century. Frequently worked by professionals as well as amateurs it has continued its popularity in the home up to the present time.

Many have discovered the pleasures of the craft. Many work on printed canvas hesitant of embarking on pattern making of their own. The patterns on the following pages have been gathered together to suggest the wide possibility of designs available. They are intended to serve as a kind of guide book, or dictionary to be referred to, but not to be copied slavishly. After working from this book I hope the reluctant designer will gain sufficient confidence to adapt and alter, and eventually to devise her own patterns. Some such element of experimentation in the hands of the embroideress keeps an enthusiasm burning which is inevitably transmitted to the embroidery.

Repeating patterns

Patterns, like music, are rhythms. The motif, however simple, when repeated becomes a pattern. A square or a line repeated becomes a check or a stripe pattern. It is a delicate balance between an interesting repeating pattern and a boring, monotonous one. With exact repetition a simple pattern is in danger of becoming obvious and tedious, while in an over-elaborate pattern the rhythm can be lost. Some element of the unexpected is needed, while retaining the simplicity.

A check pattern may be made up of a square which overlaps the next square slightly or has a piece missing. A stripe pattern may be cut up and put together again in steps. Graph paper provides a simple way of building up geometric patterns. Squares or stripes will lead on to triangles and octagons, and shapes made up from parts of these put together. It is a help to use colour to shade in areas of light and dark, and to see the pattern in terms of solid colour not line.

Geometry

Though on fine canvas most shapes are possible, when designing it is important to consider the limitations of the material. The stitches best suited to can-vas work fall naturally into horizontal, vertical and diagonal directions. There are so many permutations of these that it is more logical to build designs starting with these geometric foundations than to think up a shape first and then try to trim it to fit the canvas. Many stitches automatically fit rectangles, squares, and diamonds (that is, squares on end). These are not necessarily true squares as discrepancies in the weaving of the canvas may cause the vertical threads to be closer to one another than the horizontal, and so a diamond or parallelogram is produced.

With simple stitches, true diagonals can be produced just by stepping up one thread of canvas in each successive row. Stitches giving true diagonals include tent, gobelin, straight and web stitches. They will make chevrons, herring-bone patterns, etc.

Diagonals combined with verticals or horizontals, will give triangles, parallelograms or composite shapes, for example, arrowheads, star shapes, octagons, letter forms, etc.

Octagons using 2 vertical, 2 horizontal and 4 diagonal lines give scope for patterns. They are also good substitutes for circles, though with a larger scale of pattern to canvas, it is possible to achieve more subtle curves.

Straight stitches can be used to give curved effects even on a coarse scale. See, for example, the waves and stripes pattern, shown in figures 2, 2a and 2b, or the leopard's spots pattern, shown in figures 13 and 13a.

Some stitches will give more acute angles than that of 45 degrees, for example, encroaching gobelin stitch, and knotted stitch; and rep stitch which gives an angle of 22 degrees approximately. The angle of the first two stitches mentioned can vary depending on the number of threads covered in relation to the encroachment of one row over the next. These angles give more scope for unusual patterns in that long narrow diamond shapes can be produced. Patterns that are best avoided are those based on angles of 60 degrees; these include equilateral triangles and hexagons. There does not appear to be a stitch that falls naturally into this angle. Many stitches can be arranged in steps rising at given intervals which will give the effect of acute or obtuse angles and which can be arranged in chevrons or lozenge patterns.

The following definitions may be helpful. An equilateral triangle is one in which all sides and angles are equal. A right-angled triangle is, in this context, a square halved diagonally. A parallelogram is a figure in which opposite sides are equal and parallel. A diamond, or lozenge, has all sides of equal length, and opposite angles equal. An octagon is an eight-sided shape.

Colour

When describing colour, 'tone' means lightness or darkness in any hue, so that though the hue may be different, say, blue or brown, the tone, that is weight or darkness, can be equal. 'Shade' is probably a more familiar word, and means virtually the same thing. One of the more seductive qualities of canvas embroidery is the ease with which colours may be graded softly from dark to light. Of the tapestry wools available Appletons offer the widest range of shades.

There are no rules for using colour in canvas embroidery but the following comments may be useful as a guide. Effects of depth can be produced readily by means of shading, for flowers; and even for abstract patterns, see the shaded stripes pattern shown in figures 17 and 17a. Provided the range runs through evenly from light to dark, the hues may vary, so that a pale pink may run through heather to violet, or pale

blue may change to dark green. This slight change of hue as well as tone increases the richness of the effect. For any of the three-dimensional patterns, it is better to err on the side of sharp contrast for the strongest effects. Where flowers are used on subtler patterns, more softness of tonal contrast gives a gentler more sensitive feeling.

Colour can be essential in transforming a simple, possibly ordinary, pattern into something more inspired. Within the geometric format the colour can be repeated in another rhythm. Compare the effect of a chevron pattern when worked in two strongly contrasted shades, used in alternate stripes with the same pattern worked in many different colours used at random. Colours which repeat at regular intervals within a given format can enrich it, or one pattern can be superimposed upon another as counterpoint in music: spots against chevrons, or flowers against stripes.

Most of the simpler patterns in this book are universal, belonging to no one period of history, and no one country. They are common to all cultures. They are shown here with various possible amendments so that the embroideress can continue to experiment with them herself. Designing increases awareness. Everything looked at suggests a pattern: iron railings, rows of cakes, slatted shelves, soap bubbles, tiled floors, etc. If these are found too difficult to work on, there is all the wealth of historic ornament: stone carving in old churches, oriental rugs, primitive weaving, and, of course, old samplers. Motifs, borrowed or devised, can be drawn up on graph paper and then worked out on samplers. I have not included Florentine patterns as there are several books which deal solely with this aspect of canvas work.

Stitches

Stitches are important in that they form

the very substance of the fabric. Without doubt, the smaller and closer the stitching, the harder the wear it can take, and the slower it is to work. Long stitches that can be worked up quickly have their place for fashion accessories, decorative cushions, bags, etc., where hard wear is not a consideration. It is probably more rewarding for a beginner to start with a pattern that grows quickly using simple straight stitches.

Of the wide choice of straight, interlocking, or tying down stitches, tent stitch is deservedly the most popular. Because it can be worked more finely than any other, it allows for the greatest detail and flexibility of design. Many of the patterns on the following pages use this stitch, particularly the flower motifs and lettering, which are more fully described later. Another virtue of tent stitch is that it can be worked in different sizes. Size of stitch depends on scale of article: for a floor rug or curtain pelmet, the largest scale of stitch; for a purse or spectacle case, the smallest. Whether large or small, the area covered must allow enough room for the design to speak. Design and stitch are closely allied, though a bold design, as for upholstery, could be worked on a fine scale for durability.

Each stitch has its own character which can look well used alone, or contrasted with areas of another stitch to give more depth to the texture. The use of too many varied stitches on one piece of work tends to make it look jumbled and ragged.

Uses of canvas work

There are so many uses for which canvas work is supremely suitable that it seems pointless to make inappropriate things for the sake of it. The kind of fabric a hard-wearing stitch most resembles is light-weight carpet. It is therefore ideal for upholstery, small rugs, chair seats, stool tops, kneelers, and cushions. A less closely worked stitch will make good bags; work bags, Gladstone bags, envelope bags, duffle bags, bags on frames, and, of course, cushion covers. Softer, finer stitching, using wool, silk or stranded cotton, lends itself to clothing accessories, belts, slippers, cuffs, yokes, purses, cases for needles, silks or spectacles.

Before embarking on any piece of embroidery which is to be used for a specific purpose the method of construction must be fully worked out, so that it is in character with the embroidery. The decoration or embroidery also should be designed to fit the over-all shape of the article, not the other way about. It is usually well worth the trouble of making a sampler to discover exactly how the stitch or pattern works out before starting on the finished piece.

Craftsmanship

There needs to be a touch of the fanatic about an embroideress because so much is expected of her. She must be able to count accurately, which is more difficult than might be supposed. She must be conscientious enough to check and cross check, particularly when working repeating patterns. She needs a rhythm of working so that the actual stitching itself becomes a pattern of movements, and also she requires a certain relentlessness of purpose to see the work through to the end. Lest all this should sound too daunting there is tremendous pleasure to be found in the work. Well designed and well executed canvas embroidery can be incomparable, and much richer and more individual than anything to be bought.

Methods

The old adage is true that to do a thing

the proper way is quickest in the end. Canvas embroidery is best done on a frame. It helps prevent the work being pulled out of shape, and it makes possible a better and more even tension of stitch. With the left hand working from the front and the right hand returning the needle from the back it is much quicker to do. This is not to say that all canvas work done in the hand is no good. It is often practical to have a piece of work that is portable and can be picked up in the train, or the waiting-room. Provided it is a small piece, it can usually be pulled back to shape at the end.

Canvas comes in a variety of sizes of mesh and it is vital to choose the appropriate size for the stitch. There should be no chink of canvas showing through when the piece has been worked or it will look mean and thread-bare. On the other hand, if the canvas is too fine the stitch will look bumpy and uneven, as though it has not room to sit down.

As the thickness of tapestry wool is fairly constant, the following table may be used as a guide to the suitability of stitch to canvas:
Straight stitches, vertical or horizontal — 32 or 36 single threads to 5 cm
Tent stitch — 32 single threads to 5 cm
Tent stitch with tramé — 20 double threads to 5 cm
Fine tent stitch for silk or crewel wool — 48 single threads to 5 cm
Diagonal stitches (longer than tent) — 28 or 32 single threads to 5 cm.

For those more conversant with working in inches, this gauge simply represents double the more familiar numbers of 14, 16 or 18 threads to the inch, 5 cms being the equivalent of 2 in.

Rug wool of the type known as Sudan can be used on double canvas 14 threads to 5 cm for a coarse effect. Knitting wools can also be used when a special effect such as random dyeing is required. Some double knitting wools are equal in thickness to tapestry wool, but they should be tried first on a sampler.

Transferring designs

Though the patterns here are represented by diagrams which have to be followed stitch by stitch, there are other methods of transferring designs to canvas. Where a geometric pattern follows the straight or true diagonal grain, tacking lines can be used. These are particularly useful for a large pattern such as slanting ladders (see figures 55 and 55a). The spaces between the tacked lines may be measured accurately, or better still, counted out in threads. Tacking provides a simple, clean method of marking out border lines. Where a symmetrical shape is required a tacking line running through the centre can help ensure that each side is built up equally.

Squared paper or graph paper pro-vides one of the simplest methods of drawing up patterns. Little geometric patterns are easy to colour in with felt pens and to follow when stitching. With a more elaborate design, it may be necessary to draw it first on plain paper. If the paper is placed on glass, and lit from behind, the canvas can be placed over it, and the design painted on directly with thin oil paint or waterproof ink. Alternatively, the drawing can be traced on to squared paper. This is slower and there may be difficulty in finding the right size of graph paper for the design. Graph paper is easily obtainable in 5 or 10 squares per cm.

The finished size can be assessed from the drawing on graph paper by counting the number of squares and dividing by the number of threads per in. or 5 cm. For example, if the design measures 360 squares, to a count of 18 threads per in. or 36 per 5 cm,

$\dfrac{360}{18} = 20$ in., or $\dfrac{360}{36} \times 5 = 50$ cm. The following method can be used to work out the size of the drawing to fit an article of say 14 in. or 35 cm, using a canvas of 16 threads per in. or 32 per 5 cm: $14 \times 16 = 224$ squares or

$$35 \times \dfrac{32}{5} = 224 \text{ squares.}$$

Diagrams

The diagrams which show the patterns on the following pages are of two kinds. For every stitch except tent stitch the diagram shows the shape of the stitch, and the background grid represents the threads of the canvas. Where tent stitch is represented, the squares of the diagram depict the stitches. The grid lines are not the threads of canvas but simply the end of one stitch and the beginning of the next.

For the most part confusion only arises where tent stitch is combined with other stitches. When working from a diagram on graph paper it is a help to mark out a centre line on to the canvas with tacking stitches. If stitched from the centre outwards, the pattern can be kept evenly balanced.

Frames

Adjustable frames are the best because the canvas can be tightened from time to time as work progresses. See figure 1. They are more expensive than the simpler slate frames which are quite adequate.

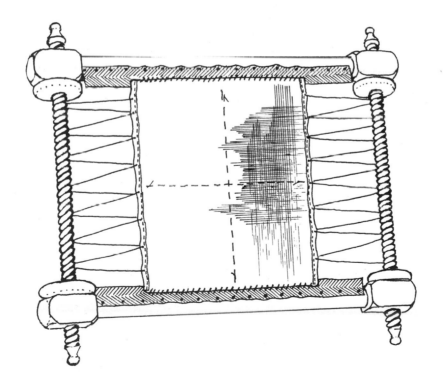

1   Adjustable frame

To dress a frame allow at least 5cm of spare canvas around the design. This amount is necessary during stretching afterwards. Bind the edges of the canvas with tape to prevent them fraying. This also acts as a cover to the rough edge of the canvas which can catch on the wool and even more on silk and roughen it. Match the centre of the canvas to the centre of the webbing on the horizontal rollers at top and bottom of the frame, and stitch in place with small, over-casting stitches. Position the rollers on the upright slats or screw bars of the frame so that the maximum tautness is achieved, and screw or peg in place. Draw the free, vertical edges of the canvas outwards lacing them to the upright slats or bars with strong thread.

Points to remember when stitching

A blunt ended needle is essential. It should be large enough to thread easily, and to pull through the canvas comfortably. Use a short thread as long threads wear thin. Always cut wool, never break it. Knots are thick and ugly, so run the thread through the stitching at the back when starting work. When starting from nothing, work over the end of the wool holding it in place, until one or two stitches have secured it. Stab stitch from front to back and then back to front in two movements. Picking up threads of canvas in the needle makes the work uneven. Work the ends into the back of the stitching. Always work in a good light.

Geometric patterns

Waves and stripes

One of the simplest patterns to work, this wavy line effect is one that can be developed in many ways. See figures 2a, 2b and 2c. Each vertical straight stitch must always cover the same number of threads, in this case 5. Three stitches are worked in line, the next is up 1 thread, the next up 2 threads, up 2 again and then up 1 to give 3 stitches in line again. As many shades as possible of 1 colour may be used to give a light to dark effect or the wavy line may be made up of 3 shades repeated twice.

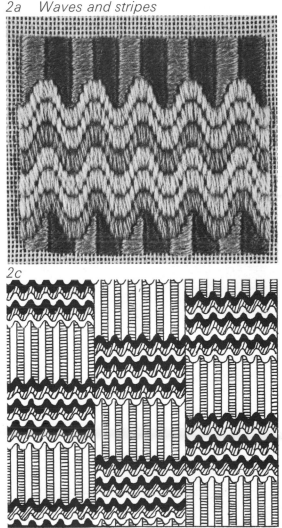

2a   Waves and stripes

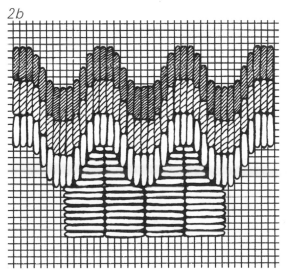

2b

2c

The whole piece of work can be just waves, or blocks of wavy lines can be interspersed with stripes of light and dark of another colour, as shown here. See figure 2a. For the straight stripes, the horizontal stitch covers six threads, and runs from the centre of one flat end of the wave to the centre of the next. To get the best cover, a single canvas 36 threads to 5 cm is used but 32 threads would do. This pattern works up quite quickly.

Zigzag

Based on one of the simplest patterns this covers quickly and is easy to work. Instead of formal chevrons which repeat exactly, these zigzag lines vary in width and length to give a random pattern. See figures 3a and 3b. It is worked entirely in straight horizontal stitches which are stepped up one thread each time to give a true diagonal line. Along each diagonal the stitches must cover the same number of threads. Where the diagonal changes direction the number of threads covered may be reduced or increased. Stitches could vary in length from 3 to 6 threads. For the most part each zigzag line can follow the one before using a different shade. Here and there a break in the formation will cause diamonds or parallelograms to appear. This is a pattern that need not be followed exactly, the irregularity being a feature of it. A formal border such as the key pattern (see figures 25a and 25b) would be appropriate. This is not the hardest-wearing stitch and covers single canvas 36 threads to 5 cm adequately.

Hinges

One unit reminiscent of a door hinge shape, interlocks with itself to give an all-over pattern. The hinge shape consists of 10 vertical stitches: 2 stitches over 2 threads, 4 stitches over 4 threads

3a Zigzag

3b

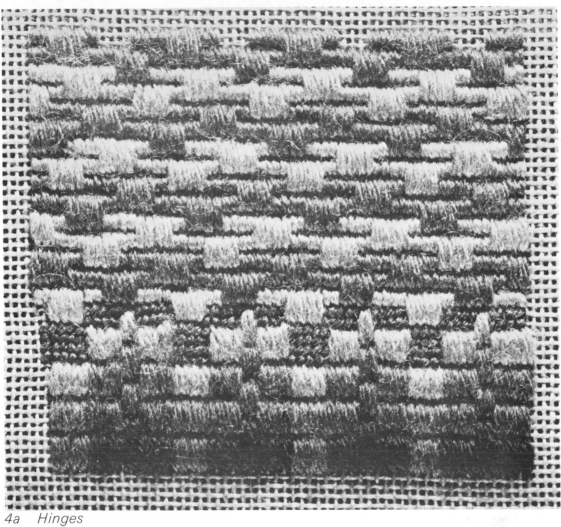

4a   Hinges

and then 4 stitches over 2 threads. All
the shapes in each row are worked in
the same colour, and 4 colours are
needed to keep the colours isolated from
each other. See figures 4a and 4b. In the
border, the shape alters slightly: 4
stitches over 4 threads, 2 stitches up 2
threads and over 4, and then 4 stitches
over 4 threads again. Several rows of
this shape can be built up, shading from
light to dark. The space between border
and ground pattern can be filled with
tent stitch. On single canvas, 36 or 32
threads to 5 cm, this pattern is neat and
small in scale, and would be suitable for
purses, spectacles cases, etc.

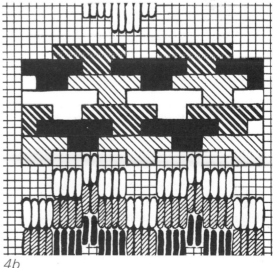

4b

Diagonal diabolo

A single unit similar to a diabolo shape
is repeated to form a pattern with a
strong diagonal slant. The unit is made
up of 24 vertical stitches. They cover
1, 2, 3, 4, 5, and then 6 threads 4 times;
up 1 thread for 2 stitches, up 2 threads
once, up another 2 threads, up 2 threads
again for 2 stitches, up 1 thread for 4
stitches and then the stitches decrease in
size over 5, 4, 3, 2 and 1 threads. See
figures 5a, 5b and 5c. The rows of units
working from top to bottom are all in
line. This is a pattern where choice of
colour can alter its character. Further
repeating patterns can be produced by
using the same colour sequence, or
random use of colour can reduce the
formality of the pattern. Once the thread
intervals have been grasped, it is a
quick pattern to work on single canvas
of 36 or 32 threads to 5 cm.

5a   *Diagonal diabolo*

Interlocking spurs

A neat little pattern of two basic shapes
which can change its character
according to the colour arrangement.
The spur shape is worked in vertical
stitches, first over 1 thread, then over
2, 3, 4, 5 and 4 threads. There are then
10 stitches over 3 threads, and then a
reverse peak is formed over 4, 5, 4, 3, 2
and 1 threads. See figure 6a. The next
spur interlocks into the peak of the last
one. A parallelogram of 6 by 6 threads
appears at the end of each spur. This is
filled with horizontal stitches. The
samplers here show respectively the
different effects obtained by irregular use
of colour, and formal repeats using 4
colours. See figures 6c and 6d. In the
diagrams the colours are used in groups
of 3 spurs of each colour, with all the
parallelograms in the same colour. On
single canvas 36 threads to 5 cm, this is
a fairly quick pattern to work and would
combine well with a rich border.

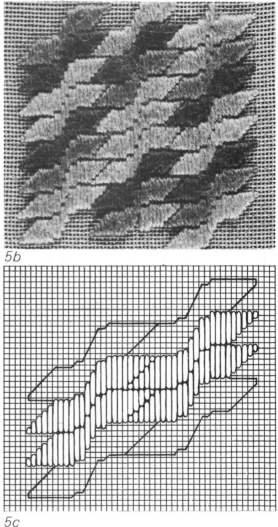

5b

5c

18

6a   *Interlocking spurs*

6b

6c

6d

Parquet floor

Parallelograms arranged horizontally and vertically make up this traditional pattern. By means of colour, further patterns can be built up within this format, e.g., chevrons, or three dimensional effects of steps, or a multi-colour random effect can be used filling in each parallelogram with a different colour. See figures 7a, 7b and 7c. A choice of two sizes of shape are shown in figures 7d and 7e for large or small pieces of work. In figure 7d, the stitches travel first over 1 thread, then 2, 3, 4 and 5 threads. There are 8 stitches over 6 threads, and then the shape decreases 5, 4, 3, 2 and 1, towards the opposite corner. In figure 7f, it increases in size to 10 threads which cover 10 times before decreasing.

Once mastered, this is an easy pattern to do, and covers fairly quickly. It can be worked on single canvas, 36 or 32 threads to 5 cm. With the latter, it is probably necessary to insert little back stitches to hide the threads which may show between the shapes. It is not a very hard-wearing stitch. A development of this pattern is shown in figure 7f. Spots worked in tent stitch are placed at irregular intervals over the parquet floor effect. It is easiest to do the spots first, and then fit in the parallelograms, making sure the overall pattern continues undistorted. Here the background was worked in several close toned shades of one colour with the spots in various shades of a contrasting colour.

Pyramids

The combination of different stitches gives this pattern an interesting surface texture. Blocks of each stitch are arranged in a pyramidal pattern. See figures 8a and 8b. The stitches used are web stitch, herring-bone, knitting stitch and velvet stitch, and they are worked

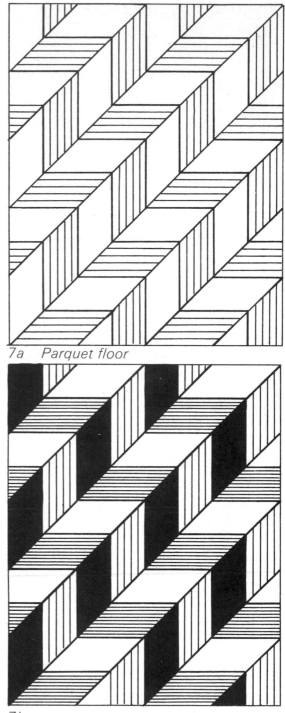

7a   Parquet floor

7b

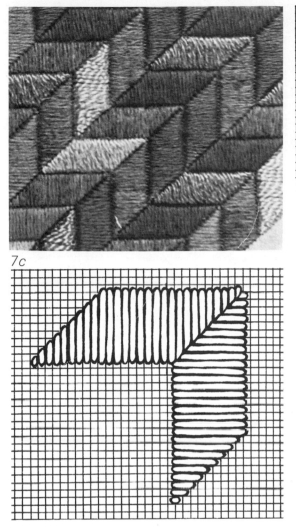

7c

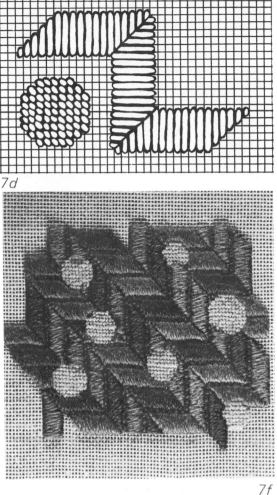

7d

7e

7f

on double canvas, 20 threads to 5 cm. Horizontally, the design is divided into 7 rows each 13 threads high. Each block of stitches is constant in width as it travels up the pattern moving in towards the centre with each step. The blocks vary in width from each other, the numbers above and below figure 8a indicating the number of threads contained in each one. The blocks which are heavily outlined are better worked in darker colours.

The different stitches, in terms of shading, are shown in the key for figure 8b. The colour remains constant in each row of stepped blocks, although

slight variation of shade could be an advantage. It is a pattern which could be doubled in size to give a diamond instead of a pyramidal structure. This is a useful pattern for those keen to try different stitches, and is fairly easy to follow. It is shown made up as a cushion in plate 3.

Sinking triangles

Triangles shaded from light to dark in 3 colours, and inverted every alternate row suggest shapes that are continually being submerged. See figures 9a and 9b. Each triangle starts from 1 stitch at

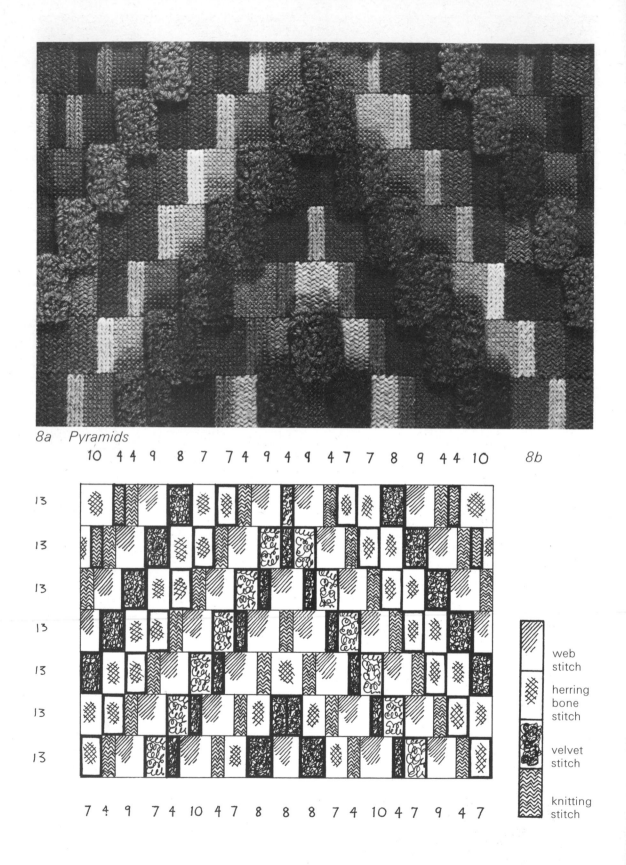

8a Pyramids

10 4 4 9 8 7 7 4 9 4 9 4 7 7 8 9 4 4 10   8b

13
13
13
13
13
13
13

7 4 9 7 4 10 4 7 8 8 8 7 4 10 4 7 9 4 7

web stitch	
herring bone stitch	
velvet stitch	
knitting stitch	

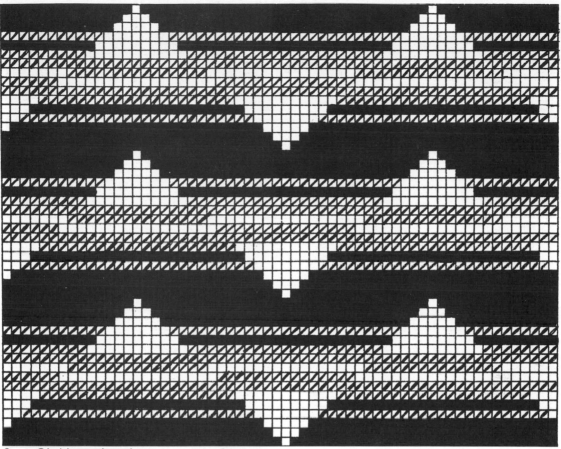

9a   *Sinking triangles*

9b

the apex, and increasing by 1 stitch at the end of every row continues for a total of 16 rows until it is 31 stitches wide. The same triangle, inverted, automatically fits the shapes left between the first row of triangles. The stripes of a medium shade on the first row of triangles should not coincide with those on the inverted row or the effect of a shape breaking through the surface will be lost. Worked all in tent stitch this pattern would be suitable for a larger area, possibly upholstery, and could be used for various sizes of mesh of canvas.

Misprints

A formal little pattern is suggested by printing faults when two colours do not register exactly. See figures 10a and 10b. This is an easy pattern to work and could be used to break up a large area of background, as in the cushion in figure 10b. It was worked in cross stitch for the cushion but could equally well be done in tent stitch on any scale of canvas. It is a thin pattern on its own

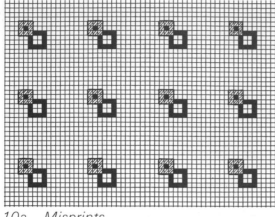

10a *Misprints*

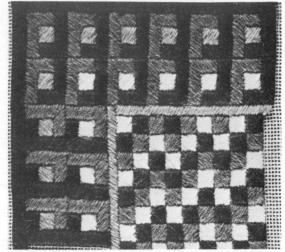

11a *Chequerboard*

10b

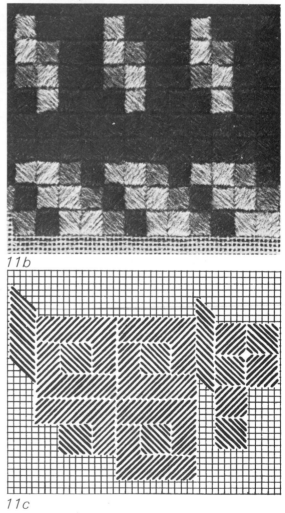

11b

and needs a richer border or centre piece to complement it.

Chequerboard

Scotch stitch provides the format for this pattern. When worked in one colour this stitch lights to give a criss-cross texture. By using several colours, a wide variety of simple geometric patterns is possible, for example, check patterns, diagonally stepped patterns, chevrons, patterns based on simplified letter forms, etc. A random arrangement of many

11c

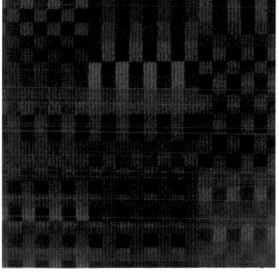

top   *The colours are used without any repeating order in this simple pattern of triangles. There is a large square within the design which is perceptible only by being predominantly blue. The canvas is very fine, approximately 48 threads to 5 cm (2 in.), and crewel wool and silk are used for the embroidery. Such a small piece of work would be suitable for a spectacle case or pencil case.*

above left   *Shaded stripes.*

above right   *The pyramids pattern shown in figures 8, 8a and 8b is used for the cushion with a long fringe. This fringe is made by looping long threads of wool into the canvas at the edge of the embroidery. The threads are either bound or are just wrapped with another thread. What is left of the thread is then spun tightly between the fingers until the ends twist up on themselves. They are then threaded back into the binding.*

Scotch stitch arranged in repeating chevrons makes the mirror frame. It is worked on single canvas 36 threads to 5 cm (2 in.).

top   *Basket of flowers.*

above left   *The design of the squab cushion was suggested by a hydrangea flower. It is worked on double canvas 20 threads to 50 cm (20 in.), in tent stitch. A border of single flowers makes the gusset which has been invisibly seamed at the corners to make a continuous strip. The cushion is piped and backed with satin.*

above right   *Velvet stitch is used for areas of thick texture on the next cushion which is described in the patches of turf pattern, shown in figures 54 and 54a. It is edged with a ready-made woollen fringe.*

11d 11e

12a

colours can give a rich mosaic effect. See figures 11a, 11b, 11c, 11d and 11e. Figure 11a shows the development of a border that gives a slightly three-dimensional effect. Diagonal stitches are worked to make a frame effect around each little square. In any deviation such as this from the set format of Scotch stitch it is important to keep an almost equal balance of diagonal stitches in each direction to keep the canvas from being pulled out of shape. Provided mistakes are not made in the direction of the stitching, this is an easy pattern to work and covers fairly quickly. Single canvas, either 36 or 32 threads to 5 cm, is suitable, and the stitch is reasonably hard-wearing.

Rooftops

A repeat made up of one self-interlocking shape (see figure 12b), this pattern appears to alter in format according to the colours used. The shape consists of a parallelogram with a triangular piece taken from one side and added to the opposite side. It is worked entirely in web stitch on double canvas of 20 threads to 5 cm. Working from the base the diagonal stitch covers 6 by 6 threads, then 5 by 5, 4 by 4 and 3 by 3, over 6 by 6 again, 6 times, then 7 by 7, 8 by 8 and 9 by 9. See figure 12b. This shape is repeated interlocking with itself to give an all-over pattern with a diagonal slant effect. In the sampler (see figure 12a), 4 colours were used in the area on the left in 2 stripes of alternately light and dark shapes. The rest of the pattern was worked in diagonal pairs of 2 light and 2 dark shapes with occasionally an odd colour to break the regularity. This colour arrangement was devised for an envelope bag, the colour change taking place along the fold of the flap.

Leopard's spots

Spots of varying sizes are set against soft stripes and bordered by a shaded wavy line pattern. See figures 13a and 13b. The spots are worked in strongly contrasted pale and dark shades, some dark at the centre, others light. The centres are then surrounded by an edging of the contrast shade with sometimes an outline around that again. Straight stitches are used for these spots which are oval or heart-shaped. They are scattered irregularly over a background of brick stitch, worked in 2

12b   Rooftops

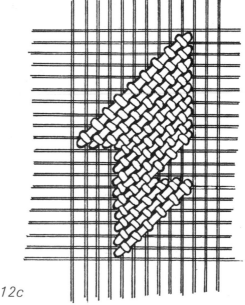

12c

26

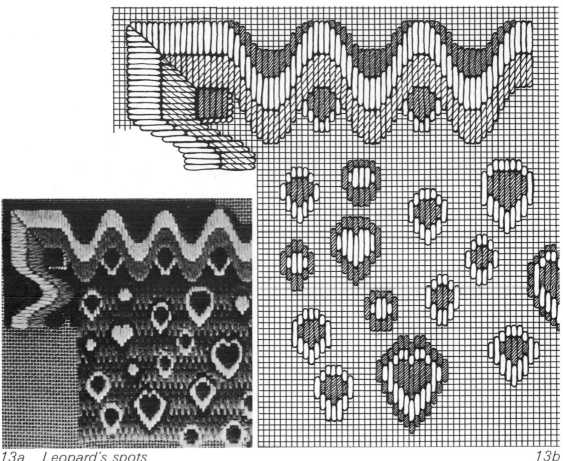

13a   Leopard's spots   13b

closely graded shades in alternate rows.
The brick stitches cover 4 threads each
time. In the border of wavy lines, the
stitches cover 6 threads. Starting from
the bottom, 3 stitches are worked in line.
The next 2 stitches each step up 1
thread, then 3 stitches step up 2 threads
each time, 2 more stitches step up 1
thread each, and then 2 more in line
with the last make the top of the wave.
See figure 13.

This is a more elaborate version of the
wavy line pattern shown in figures 2a,
2b and 2c. The spaces between the
curves of the waves on the inside edge
are filled with spots. Corners in this

border can be negotiated by straighten-
ing the curves of the waves and
bringing each side to meet on a true
diagonal. The sampler shown in figure
13a was worked in pale pink, chocolate
brown and two shades of pinky brown
on single canvas, 36 threads to 5 cm.
The finer canvas is necessary for a good
cover, but with so many long stitches
the work is not slow.

Basket weave

This pattern (see figures 14 and 14a) is
used for the basket of flowers design
shown in plate 2. Three colours, light,

14a Basket weave
14b

medium and dark are needed. As well as depicting a container for flowers or fruit, this pattern can be used as an all-over background pattern. It will make a wide border to frame other designs. Worked all in tent stitch it is suitable for any scale of canvas.

Little stars

Star shapes worked in straight vertical stitches stand away from a tent stitch background. See figures 15a and 15b. Two colours may be used alternately for the stars, or they may follow diagonal lines in a more complex colour sequence. Each star is made up of 8 stitches over 1, 2, 6, 5, 5, 6, 2 and 1 threads. The spacing is the same between every alternate row of stars. See figure 15a. The background is filled in afterwards in tent stitch. A border of lines and triangles can be built up with diagonal stitches, keeping the slanting direction equally balanced from left and right to keep the canvas in shape. This is quite a small scale pattern, suitable for single canvas 32 or 36 threads to 5 cm. Worked all in tent stitch it could be reproduced on a larger scale.

Petrol stains

This design (see figures 16a and 16b) was suggested by the variegated colour effects produced when petrol is spilt on a wet road. Similar shapes and streaks of colour can be seen when light is refracted by thick glass or water. As the forms are so inconstant and irregular, the diagram (see figure 16a) is intended as a guide only, and may be freely inter-preted; so spreading a shape is difficult to follow, and accurate counting is not essential. The tent stitch blobs could be arranged in stripes similar to watered silk, or they may be scattered freely to

15a   Little stars

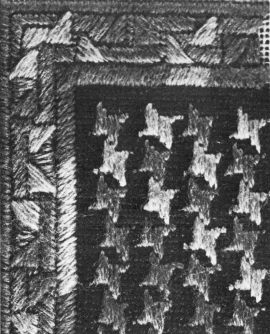

15b

fill a square or round shape. Use of
colour is all important. The juxtaposition
of one brilliant colour against another
can give a dazzling effect as in a prism.

In the sampler (see figure 16b), the
centre of each blob is shaded from pale
to rose pink, around this a ring of
yellow, then turquoise outlined by a
narrow edge of purple, then a broken
line of scarlet, and finally a shadow all
around of soft mauve broken by
blotches of brown. These blobs are set
against a background of Byzantine
stitch in shades of pale terra cotta.
Varying the combination of shades
breaks the monotony of the background
and helps to link one set of coloured
blobs with another. The feather border
(shown in figure 24) is also broken by
variations in the colour. Single canvas of
32 threads to 5 cm is the most appro-

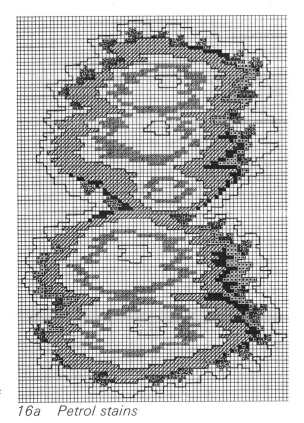

16a   Petrol stains

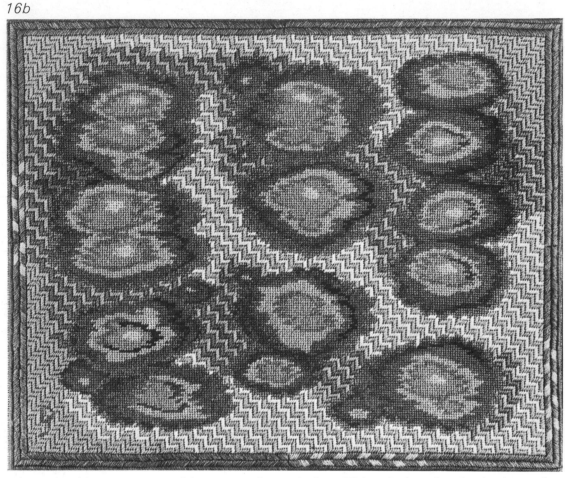

priate. As this pattern provides scope for much alteration and development, it is not recommended for beginners.

Shaded stripes

Evenly graded shades of each colour give this pattern an illusion of depth in space. See figures 17a and 17b. The design is based on units of 4. Each square is made up of 4 stripes of one colour alternating with 4 stripes of another. Each colour is divided into 4 shades. All the 12 squares of the design are worked on this basic principle, using 3 main colours. Each square covers 32 by 32 double threads of canvas of 20 double threads to 5 cm.

Each stripe is 4 double threads wide. Rep stitch is used throughout the design. This stitch splits the horizontal double thread to give 64 stitches down the length of each square but 32 stitches across. Thus a stripe, 4 stitches wide, may be made up of 8 blocks of 8 stitches in length, or 16 blocks of 4 stitches, or possibly 2 blocks of 32 stitches. See figure 17a. One stripe may be shaded from light to dark in order 1, 2, 3, 4, 1, 2, 3, 4, while the next stripe could be shaded 4, 3, 2, 1, 2, 3, 4. Many variations of this scheme can be developed. It is best to avoid stripes of the same colour meeting where one square joins the next. Blue shaded next to red will give an effect of distance, the pale blue sinking back like the sky, and the red appearing to come forward. Even without this trick, effects of depth can be produced with shading to

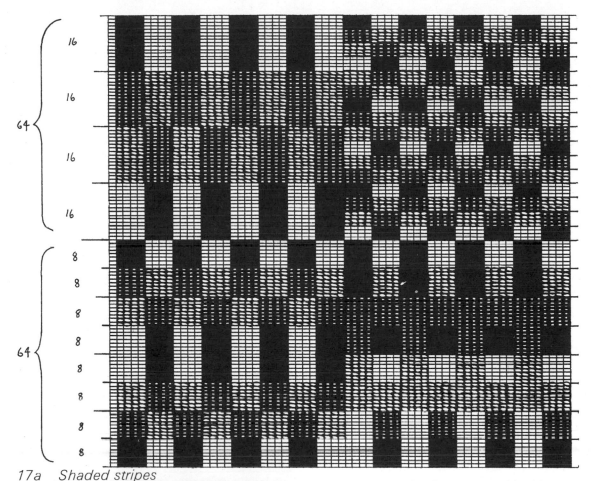

16

16

64

16

16

8
8
8
64
8
8
8
8
8

17a   Shaded stripes

suggest woven basket patterns, grid patterns, etc.

Because of its small scale this stitch is suitable for small articles such as purses, though it is hard-wearing enough for kneelers, stool tops, etc. The patterns here could be produced in any multiple of 32 threads to give long, thin shapes as well as squares. In the sampler shown in colour, each square is different, but other designs could be worked out repeating the same squares at given intervals.

17b

Three-dimensional patterns

Creating an illusion of depth in a two-dimensional medium has fascinated designers since ancient times. When achieved by very simple means it seems the more skilful, yet the trick is easy to learn. Diagonal lines which can be worked so easily on canvas give the effect of perspective when combined with vertical and horizontal lines. When the shapes thus drawn are filled with colour in strongly contrasted shades, the effect is given more weight. Cube shapes are probably the easiest to work out, and a minimum of 3 shades repeated regularly will give the required effect. Many simple flat patterns can be converted to three-dimensional ones with the addition of shadow effects. A more complex shape like a key pattern can also be worked effectively in three dimensions.

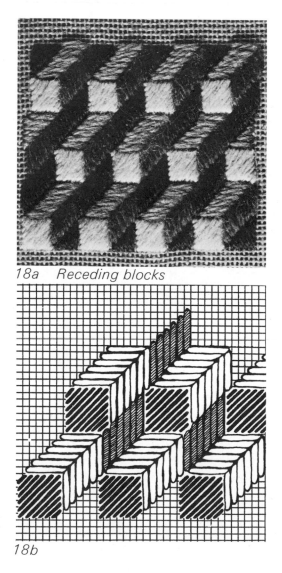

18a   Receding blocks

18b

Receding blocks

The Romans used a variation of this pattern in their mosaic floors. Parallelograms worked in 4 different shades are put together in a way that gives an effect of blocks standing up in rows which appear to recede in space. The direction of the stitching further emphasizes this effect. See figures 18a and 18b. The sampler (figure 18a) shows better than the diagram (figure 18b) the best way of using the colours, with the lightest filling the square at the front of each block. For this the stitches travel diagonally over a square 6 by 6 threads. Above this square the next palest shade is worked horizontally, 6 stitches over 6 threads going back along the diagonal. The area that makes the side of the block consists of 6 vertical stitches over 6 threads going back along the diagonal, and worked in a darker shade. This shape continues with another 6 stitches in the darkest colour to suggest a hollow underneath the next block. It is a simple, fairly quick pattern to work on single canvas 32 or 36 threads to 5 cm. It can be further developed by introducing 4 shades of another colour and picking out some of the blocks in stepped stripes.

Escalator

Worked in 4 colours this pattern gives a strongly three-dimensional effect, suggesting steps. See figures 19a and 19b. Basically, it is a pattern of light and dark vertical stripes interrupted by light and dark diagonal stripes. The dark stripes in the sampler (see figure 19a) are red and brown, and the light stripes beige and white. In length from top to bottom each block of stripes, whether vertical or diagonal, occupies 10 threads. See figure 19b.

Within a block of vertical stripes the brown stitches cover 4 threads worked horizontally, while the lighter stripes in between are filled with white diagonal stitches over 3 threads. After 4 stripes of brown and white the colours change to red and beige in the same horizontal block. In the next block, this time of diagonal lines, the brown horizontal stitches cover 3 threads with beige vertical stitches covering 4 threads. Again after 4 stripes each of brown and

beige the stripes change to red and white. The third block is as the first with brown and white and red and beige in vertical stripes. The fourth block is as the second with brown and beige and red and white in diagonal stripes. The fifth block continues as the first, except that there is a further colour change, with red and beige changing places with brown and white.

This is perhaps a tricky pattern to grasp at first, but the change of colour combined with change of direction of stripe is very important for the effect. On single canvas of 36 threads to 5 cm, this pattern needs a minimum area of approximately 20 cm by 16 cm.

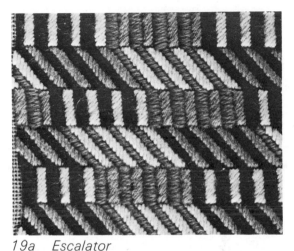

19a   Escalator

19b

20a   Twisted ribbons

20b

Twisted ribbons

This pattern (see figures 20a and 20b) is used for the embroidered mules in plate 4. It is important that the underside of the ribbon should be noticeably darker than the top side to achieve the maximum three-dimensional effect. See figure 20a. Each ribbon can be a different colour from the next or they can, as in the diagram, be of two colours in alternate rows. See figure 20b. Though the pattern was designed entirely for tent stitch, if the ribbons are worked in vertical straight stitches against a tent stitch background, they will stand out more. Single canvas of 32 threads to 5 cm is suitable for either stitch, and double canvas of 20 threads to 5 cm for tent stitch only.

Houses on a hill

This is a variation of the cube pattern so popular in patchwork. See figures 21a and 21b. Three colours that are distinct from each other, light medium and dark in tone, give the pattern a feeling of 3 dimensions. Detail developed within the diamond shapes gives the impression of roofs and chimneys and so suggests rows of houses. An extra subtlety is

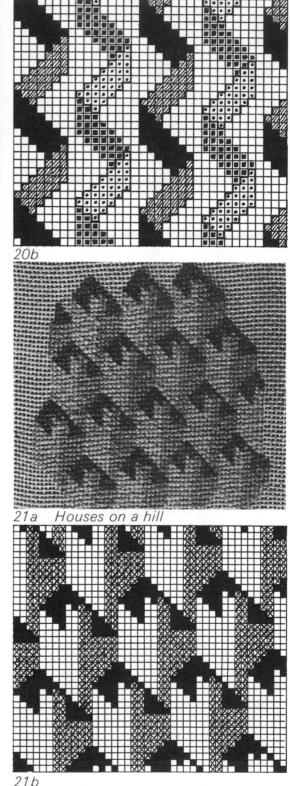

21a   Houses on a hill

21b

added in that when working from left to right each house along a horizontal line moves up one thread. This pattern can be treated as a simple all-over repeat, or variations can take place in the colour arrangements, provided the three tonal differences are kept distinct. Worked entirely in tent stitch, single canvas of 32 threads to 5 cm, or double canvas of 20 threads to 5 cm is suitable.

Trellis

Knotted stitch in zigzag lines of two shades gives a strongly three-dimensional effect similar to a trellis pattern. See figures 22a and 22b. The first zigzag line is made up of blocks of 3 rows each of 4 knotted stitches. Using the lighter shade these stitches are worked to give a right-hand slant. The second block of 3 rows of 4 stitches slants to the left and is worked in a darker shade. The next zigzag line interlocks with the first, and where it meets it, is only 2 stitches wide. The second and third rows are 4 stitches wide. Again the right-hand slant is in the lighter shade and the left-hand one in the darker. Where the second zigzag meets the first, the adjoining stitches will occupy the same holes. In the second row, the first stitch may only be a half stitch, and it may be necessary to add an extra little half stitch if any canvas shows along this join. This is not the easiest pattern to work because of the difficulty of fitting the two zigzag lines together. They must fit accurately each time or the continuity of the pattern will be lost. The diamond spaces left between these lines are filled with straight stitches. As a double canvas of 20 threads to 5 cm is used, these straight stitches must go between every thread to cover closely.

22a Trellis

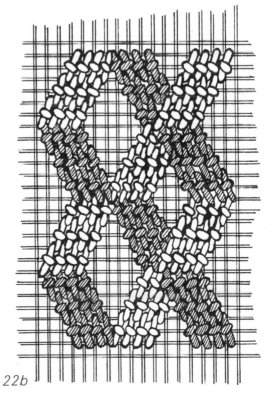

22b

Borders

A look at oriental carpets will demonstrate how much can be made of border patterns. They are probably easier to design than all-over patterns. The proportion of narrow width to long length is an interesting shape at the outset. Simple patterns, such as diagonal lines or rows of squares, take shape readily as borders, as do lines of different widths which will give variegated stripe patterns.

Basically, there are two types of border featured on the following pages: those that make continuous strips, and those where the pattern will allow for turning corners, and thus make frame shapes. Continuous strips can range from the simplest abstract patterns to the rich, intricate coiling of leaf and flower motifs. The flowing quality which a continuous line or stalk gives to a pattern becomes its own obstacle when faced with turning a corner. Such patterns in expert hands can be manoeuvred around a right angle, but there is a danger of them looking laboured. If frame shapes are required a simple all-over pattern can sometimes be more effective with, as it were, a window cut out of it, or a strip pattern made up of separate units with one of the units centred in the corner. Where formal geometric patterns are used, the change of direction must take place along the true diagonal of the canvas. A small mirror placed at an angle of 45 degrees on the border design will help in determining the best place to turn the corner.

Designs for rugs, cushions, etc., can be built up almost entirely of framed borders with very little at the centre. Set one inside another, they can range from geometric to floral in a variety of widths with a continuity of colour scheme to unite them. When arranging these various borders together it is important to check that the same mesh of canvas is suitable for all. For a combination of straight stitches and tent stitches, single canvas of 32 threads to 5 cm will probably be found the most versatile. Borders as continuous strips can be used for straps and gussets on bags, or for upholstery, or for curtain ties. Border strips making a criss-cross pattern can be used to build up a framework to contain panels of geometric patterns, or bunches of flowers. Such a format provides an inconspicuous method of joining pieces of canvas together where a large area is required, as for a carpet. On a finer scale, borders are useful for dress accessories, belts, cuffs, and hat bands. On a broader scale, wide patterns would

make good pelmets for curtains, or bed valances, or insets and panels for cushions and upholstery.

23a

Diagonal stripe

Closely worked diagonal stitches over 2 by 2 threads makes this a very hard-wearing border. See figure 23. The pattern is simply achieved by bands of colour occupying narrow or wide stripes. As the stitch is worked diagonally so the stripes run in the same direction. Brightness of texture can be produced by introducing narrow stripes worked in stranded cotton. By working another strip in the reverse direction of stitch (see figure 23b), a V shape can be produced, though this does cause the canvas to be rather pulled out of shape. As a narrow diagonal border, this pattern is eminently suitable for belts, bands, gussets on cushions, or upholstery, etc. It is a pattern that can, however, be used as an all-over design of simple diagonal stripes, or broken into chevrons. Single canvas of 32 or 28 threads to 5 cm, is most suitable.

Feather border

This is a narrow border and can be used on its own or as a final outside frame

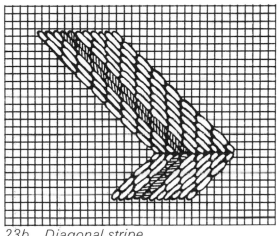

23b   Diagonal stripe

around other borders. See figure 24. It consists of 2 rows of diagonal stitches worked in opposite directions, each stitch covering 3 by 3 threads. The colours are divided into 6 dark and 4 light stitches each, and arranged as a counter change, the 4 light meeting the centre 4 dark stitches of the opposite row. In order that each corner may be treated similarly the pattern has to break at the centre of each side, so that the left-hand part is the exact reverse of the right. At the corner the light stitches of the inside row cover 5, 4, 3, 2 and 1 cross-threads, working right into the corner. On the outside edge the last

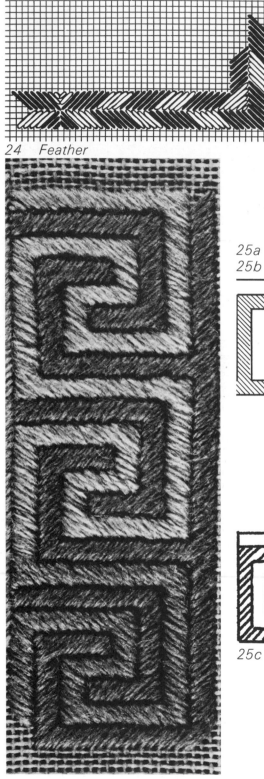

24 Feather

blocks of light stitches on either side of the corner are made up of 5 not 4 stitches each. An all-over pattern can be developed from this border which is worked on single canvas of 32 or 36 threads to 5 cm.

Key pattern

This is a simplified version of the classical Greek border. See figures 25a, 25b and 25c. Two colours are needed, though more could be used for a richer effect. See figure 25a. Basically, it is like two letters Js which interlock leav-

25a   Key pattern
25b

25c

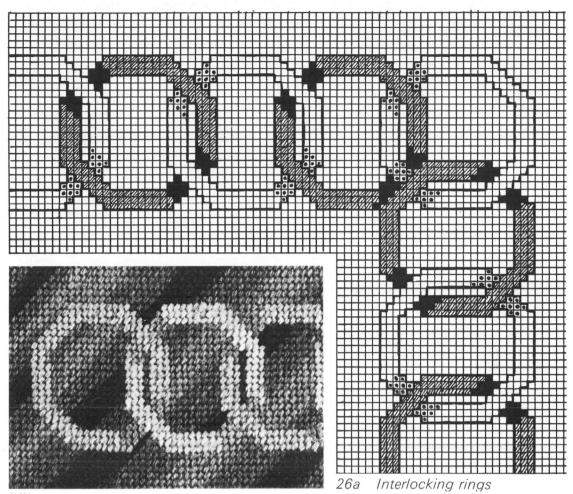

26a   *Interlocking rings*

26b

ing a broken background of the same width. It is worked in diagonal stitches covering 3 by 3 threads. The J shapes are worked in one colour with a left-hand slant and the remaining background is worked in the second colour with a right hand slant. See figure 25b. Stitched this way the canvas keeps its shape. The total width of the border is 24 threads, but an extra line of stitches on the inside edge, and possibly on the outside edge too, will give it an extra frame. When working this border for a square or rectangular shape the corner must occur at the end of a square of

pattern. The work then can quite simply be turned on end and the next side continued as before in line with the last square. See figure 25c. Single canvas of 32 or 36 threads to 5 cm is suitable, and the border could be used around a geometric or flowered centre.

Interlocking rings

A classical border which reproduces well in tent stitch. See figures 26a and 26b. Because an effect of shading is easy to work in a slightly darker colour, these rings emerge as three-dimensional shapes. Where one ring overlaps the next the effect is heightened by shading which throws forward the ring which is in front. Here the rings are coloured green and pink alternately. For the background a random dyed wool is used. By working the tent stitch in diagonal rows, an unusual, broken striped effect is produced. See figure 26b. This border makes a good gusset for a squab cushion, or a band to tie back curtains. It can be worked on single canvas, 32 threads to 5 cm, or on double canvas 20 threads to 5 cm.

Flowered border against diagonals

Tent stitch flowers against a diagonally striped background make this an appropriate border for the pattern of flowerheads against zigzag stripes (see figures 45a and 45b). It could also be used around simple geometric patterns. Each flower is worked in tent stitch with the centre possibly matching the background. See figures 27a and 27b. The stripes of the background are worked in alternate diagonal rows of vertical and horizontal stitches. The length of the stitch in each stripe may vary from row to row but must remain constant throughout each stripe, except where the flowers cut into it. If more than one colour is used for the stripes a strong contrast should be avoided or the flowers will tend to disappear.

Row of tulips

Because this tent stitch border (see figures 28a and 28b) should be viewed the right way up, its uses are limited. On a small scale of canvas it will make belts, etc., and on a larger scale, curtain ties, upholstery borders, etc.

Spider's web

Though this pattern is designed as a

27a   *Flowered border against diagonals*

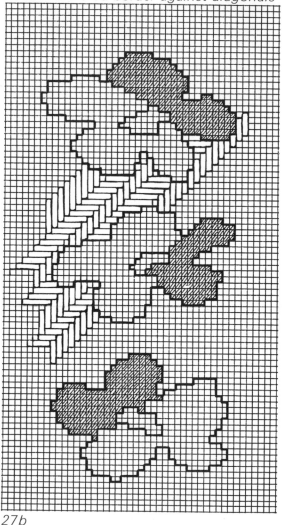

27b

40

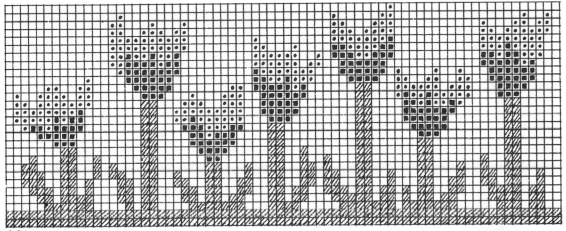

28a Row of tulips

28b

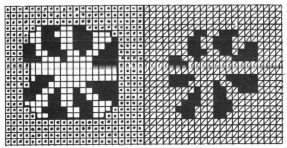

29a Spider's web

29b

stripe, because it is sub-divided into squares, it could easily be repeated to make an all-over pattern. The little squares vary in that some need 2, others 3 colours. See figures 29a, 29b and 29c. The pattern within each square is

irregular, and need not be followed exactly. Worked all in tent stitch it will make a suitable border or gusset for upholstery. As an all-over repeating pattern it can be used on a large scale for a rug. See figure 29c.

29c

30a

30b Dancing flowers   30c

Dancing flowers

These flowers appear to move because
of the irregularity of their shapes. For
this reason they are easy to work as
complete accuracy is not required. Most
of the flowers have five petals which are
outlined in a lighter or darker colour.
See figures 30a and 30b. This border is

used around the basket of flowers
design shown in plate 2a, and can make
one of a set of borders combining
geometric with flower patterns. It can
also be repeated in strips to give an
all-over pattern with a striped effect.
See figure 30c. Variety in the tonal
contrasts of flowers against background
is important for this design. As it is

worked all in tent stitch it is suitable for any scale of canvas.

Continuous leaf border

Worked in tent stitch with a leaf stitch edge (see figures 31a and 31b), this border is appropriate for the leaves pattern (see figures 52a and 52b). In the diagram the pattern is cut so that one end continues where the other end leaves off. Because it does not lend itself to easy manoeuvring around corners, this border should be added at either end of an area of leaf stitch pattern. Single canvas of 32 threads to 5 cm is best for this. When used as a border on its own it is suitable for belts, for gussets in upholstery, etc. On double canvas the leaf stitch edge is omitted, also the inside frame of diagonal stitches. Because only 3 leaves make up the motif, the tediousness of such frequent repeats can be broken by continually changing slightly the colour of leaves and stalks, and varying the background colour.

Herbaceous border

This design figure 32 is not complex. The pattern extends for two sides of the square so that each opposite side is the same. Where the diagram ends on one side it is matched exactly on the other side to give a continuous design, measuring approximately 35 cm, or 14 in. square, when worked on double canvas, 20 threads to 5 cm. The bunch of flowers in the centre is worked against the misprints background pattern shown in figures 10a and 10b. The centre line running through the bunch of flowers should be lined up with the centre line of the border. This border can also be used as a strip border for a belt or curtain tie.

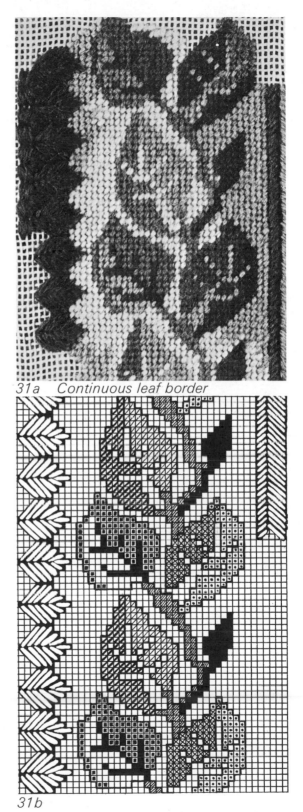

31a   Continuous leaf border

31b

33

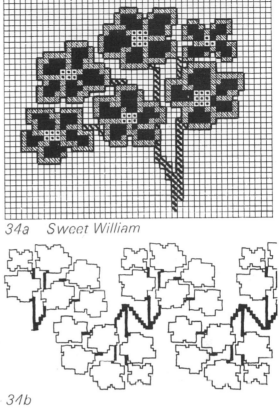

34a   *Sweet William*

34b

Continuous rose border

This tent stitch border can be worked
continuously over a long area. The
diagram represents the size of the
repeat, the one end exactly continues
the design where the other end leaves
off. See figure 33. On double canvas
20 threads to 5 cm, the repeat would
measure approximately 35 cm or 14
inches. It makes a grand pelmet to hang
above plain curtains, or, as a single
motif, it can be used as a central panel
on a velvet cushion. The open rose is
the one also shown in diagram form in

figure 35. Variety in the colours of the
leaves and stalks would add to the
richness of this design.

Sweet-william

This is a composite flower-head similar
to a sweet-william flower. See figures
34a and 34b. The petals are worked in 2
or more colours, a paler one being used
as an outline. The centres of the flowers
can be stitched in silk. This flower-head
can form part of a mixed group of
flowers or it can be used for a border.
For the latter, the flower motif is
repeated at intervals along a horizontal
line, with the spaces between filled with
the same motif inverted. A diagonal line
connects the stalks. See figure 34b. This
is a design for tent stitch on any scale of
canvas.

Flower patterns

Because of their popularity, the next chapter is devoted to flower patterns. These are not intended to belong to any historical period, though some have been developed from traditional sources, popular folk art, or grand renaissance style. One of the great attractions of working flower patterns is that they are so readily understood and enjoyed. Slight mistakes in pattern reading on the part of the embroideress are of less significance than when working a repeating pattern, as the flowers themselves can be irregular and asymmetrical in shape. It is possible for the less experienced designer to develop flower patterns from illustrations, or photographs, or from the flowers themselves. Here are a few guide lines: avoid images where the flower is seen in sharp perspective or strong light and shade. Instead work on the flat pattern quality of the plant, leaves that grow in regular, repetitive shapes, or flowers seen flat, head-on or in profile. Shading, which can be done so readily in tent stitch, can be used to good effect here. Flowerheads or petals can be worked from the centre outwards, from dark to light or light to dark. Narrow outlines, one stitch wide, can emphasize the shape.

It is worth looking at the way flowers have been treated by the embroiderers of other historical periods, or parts of the world. Sometimes the flower is so stylized that it appears as a pattern before being recognized as a flower. Whether the aim is for realistic representation or more abstract pattern, flowers must be organized first with regard to their own shapes, and then in their arrangement and relation to each other. Studying flowers, their structure and growth patterns, is a great help in understanding how to design them. Plants have a beautiful pattern quality in the arrangement of leaf and petal. Roses have a basic 5 petal structure and 7 leaves. Bramble leaves grow in groups of 5, and laburnum in groups of 3. Wild flowers demonstrate these patterns more readily than garden ones. Because plants grow in repeating patterns they lend themselves particularly well to border designs. Ivy and convolvulus are good examples where the plant can travel the length of the border on one continuous stalk. A runner bean plant twisting around a stake can be used effectively; the stake provides a rigid centre to the design. Much can also be learnt about colour from looking at plants: cabbage leaves can run from purple to green; a pale rose may flower on a deep red stalk with brown leaves; or there is the unexpected reversal of

35　Daisy heads and other flower patterns

colours in the blue stalk and green flower of a hydrangea.

Flowers can very well be combined with abstract repeating patterns, as on the cushion shown in figure 32. Such small patterns relieve the boredom of working large areas of single coloured background that often surround bunches or groups of flowers. Alternatively, a little flower motif may be repeated as a background for a much larger flower or group of flowers. If a plainer background is preferred, it is sometimes richer when worked in several close toned shades of one colour. Tent stitch is an obvious choice of stitch for flowers because of the amount of detail possible. Encroaching gobelin stitch is also suitable particularly for shading. This stitch gives a slightly raised effect when combined with tent stitch but needs a fairly big flower as it is a large stitch. French knots make good centres for flowers if worked close together. The addition of small amounts of silk can brighten a flower, either for the centre or as a narrow outline around the petals. Pearsall's embroidery silk can be bought in a single twisted thread or in strands of six threads. Six threads work in well with tapestry wool. The single twisted thread can be used double with tapestry wool, or single with crewel wool on very fine canvas. Stranded embroidery cotton is an adequate substitute for pure silk, but it does not retain its lustre so well.

Many of the flower motifs on the following pages can be used separately or in different ways from those suggested. Figure 35 gives a choice of various flower shapes that need to be organized into a pattern before they can be used. The crescent shape of flowers shown at the foot of the diagram is used on the cuff of the mule in plate 4. The other flowers appear in the basket of flowers design, shown in plate 2. If it is a rose or daisy, the same flower-head

may be used more than once. By placing it sideways on or upside down it appears slightly different. For a composite arrangement of flowers such as this, it is necessary to work out the design thoroughly on graph paper first. Balance rather than symmetry is achieved by adding sprigs of smaller flowers and leaves. The basket weave pattern, shown in figures 14a and 14b makes the basket. The arch was drawn up symmetrically on graph paper, and the marbling pattern, shown in figures 53a and 53b filled in around. A border of dancing flowers (see figures 30a, 30b and 30c) surrounds the whole, which is worked entirely in tent stitch, except for the narrow framing inside the border, which is worked in a longer diagonal stitch over 2 by 2 threads. Instead of sitting on a flat surface within an arch, the basket of flowers can float on a plain-colour background. It can also form the centre of a panel on a rug divided into panels containing different flower groups.

Geometric flowers

A formal geometric flower pattern (see figures 36a and 36b), this can be reproduced in repetitive or irregular colouring. It is a very simple pattern to follow, worked all in tent stitch on canvas or 20 or 32 threads to 5 cm. It is also a suitable pattern for a rug on double canvas 14 threads to 5 cm.

Flowered tiles

A framework of octagons contains symmetrical flowers. See figures 37a and 37b. There are two styles of flowers in two different colourings, and they are repeated alternately. A little diamond shape occurs at the corner of each octagon which helps to set off the flower shapes. To break the symmetry, colour changes can take place along

top left   *Made in the south of France in the 1920s this bag is worked in dyed raffia over a fine double canvas. The stitch is a simple interlocking straight stitch relieved by stripes of diagonal stitch. The berries are worked in French knots. This is a good example of a simple decorative pattern wholly related to the construction of the piece.*

top right   *The twisted ribbons pattern shown in figures 20 and 20a, worked in tent stitch, is used for the mules with wooden soles. The uppers are cut in two pieces to accommodate the shape of the foot. The piecing together and the edging are done with overcasting stitches over a padding of rug wool. The uppers are lined with suede and finished with a narrow suede strip through which the gimp pins are fixed into the wooden soles.*

above left   *The bag on a frame is decorated with the carpet of flowers pattern shown in figures 38 and 38a. The front and back are joined with overcasting stitches worked over rug wool. The tassles bound with silk are added afterwards.*

above right   *The nineteenth century purse is worked all in cross stitch on a fine double canvas. The pattern is a diagonal formation of block shapes, which are worked in shaded stripes. The purse is edged with a silk cord which continues into the handle. The covered button matches the lining.*

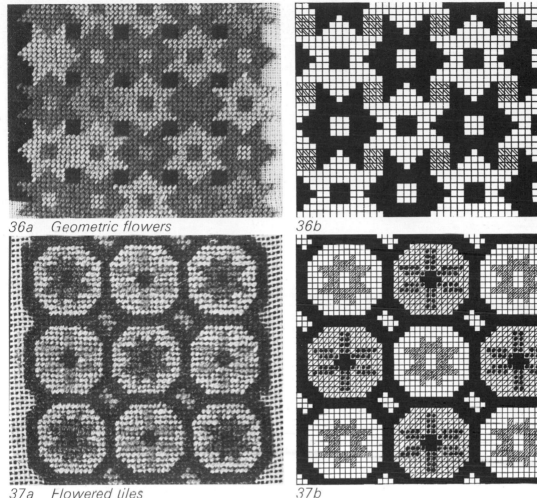

36a   Geometric flowers

36b

37a   Flowered tiles

37b

diagonal rows of flowers. Tent stitch is used entirely for this pattern, which can be reproduced on a large or small scale.

Carpet of flowers

Though the same flower shape is repeated all over, varied use of colour can make this a rich pattern. See figures 38a and 38b. The 9 petals of each flower can be worked in 2 or 3 shades or close toned colours, and set against either a lighter or darker medallion

Opposite   Scotch stitch arranged in repeating chevrons makes the mirror frame. It is worked on single canvas 36 threads to 5 cm (2 in.)

shape. These medallion shapes can only occur around every alternate flower, otherwise small gaps are left in between. Around the intervening flowers the background is taken up to meet the medallions. As the whole design is in tent stitch, it could be reproduced in a variety of different sizes, from fine canvas, 32 threads to 5 cm, for a bag (see plate 4), to coarse double canvas, 14 threads to 5 cm, for a floor rug.

Tulips

One single flower motif is repeated all over in a half drop pattern. See figures 39a and 39b. As this is a small motif it

38a   *Carpet of flowers*

38b

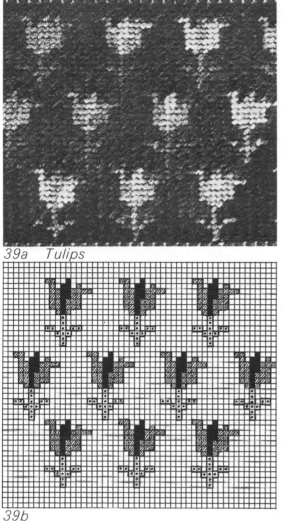

39a Tulips

39b

Milkwort

A curved sprig pattern repeats itself in reverse on alternate rows. See figures 40a and 40b. For the best effect, the pattern should contain at least 12 sprigs. Worked entirely in tent stitch, on canvas of 20 or 32 threads to 5 cm it is suitable for upholstery or cushions.

Knapweed

This formal half drop pattern of symmetrical flowers, shown in figures 41a and 41b, is worked all in tent stitch. Some variation in the colour of the

40a Milkwort

can be used for a bag or purse. It will also make a background pattern for much larger flowers. In this case it may be better to place the tulips irregularly over the background so they are not confused with the main flowers. In the sampler, shown in figure 39a, the tulips are worked in tent stitch in various colours. The ground is covered in diagonal stitches over 2 by 2 threads, which are worked in vertical rows. Single canvas 32 threads to 5 cm can be used, but if the design is worked all in tent stitch, double canvas 20 threads to 5 cm is suitable.

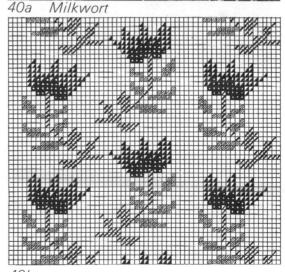

40b

41a Knapweed

41b

42 Artichoke

52

flowers prevents the repeat from becoming monotonous. The colour change can be introduced along diagonal lines of flowers. This makes a good upholstery pattern on canvas of 20 or 32 threads to 5 cm.

Artichoke

A rather baroque flower this (see figure 42), which can be used singly or in a repeating pattern. It can also be included in a mixed flower design as in basket of flowers, shown in plate 2. Worked all in tent stitch, it is suitable for canvas of 20, 32, or 36 threads to 5 cm.

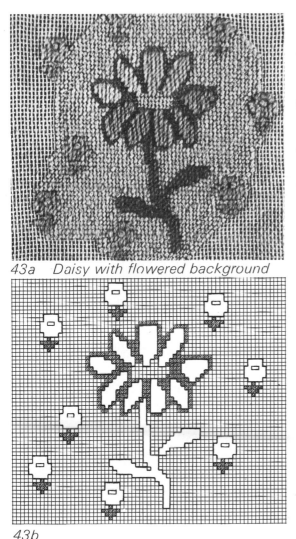

43a   Daisy with flowered background

43b

Daisy with flowered background

The daisy can form the central motif for a small bag, etc., or it could be worked as a repeating pattern to cover a larger area. See figures 43a and 43b. The petals, stalk and leaves are worked in encroaching gobelin stitch covering 2 by 1 threads. This gives a slightly raised effect, which is further emphasized by the outline of the petals and the centre of the flower being worked in tent stitch in silk or stranded cotton. The flowers of the background are also worked in encroaching gobelin with a French knot at the centre, and the stalk in tent stitch. The flowers are scattered freely over the background which is also in tent stitch. If used as a repeating motif, allow twice the width of the daisy in background between the daisies, moving horizontally. In the next row the daisies can be fitted centrally in the spaces between the previous row of daisies. This row should start about 10 threads down from the ends of the stalks of the previous row. Worked on single canvas of 32 threads to 5 cm, this gives a hard-wearing surface suitable for upholstery.

Aubretia against stripes

This pattern (see figure 44) and the next (see figure 45) form a pair, and can be used, for example, for two cushions of similar size and shape. Tent stitch flowers against a background of straight stitches give an interesting variety of texture. The straight stitches are worked in alternate diagonal rows of horizontal and vertical. In the sampler shown in figure 44, two shades of beige are used, but a contrast of shade will emerge if the same colour is used, as the light strikes differently on each direction of stitch. It is easiest to work the tent stitch flowers first. The diagram (see figure 44) can be used as a general guide to their positions. For working a larger area, continue to place them irregularly, not necessarily repeating exactly either their shape or their position. The flower centres can be worked in silk or stranded cotton. The background or straight stitches is then filled by working in diagonal rows, cutting them short where necessary to fit around the flowers. The diagonal lines must be kept true as they weave around the flowers, or much of the effect will be lost. In the border the straight stitches are worked diagonally, alternating their direction, to give a herring-bone effect.

The inside edge of the border looks well if broken occasionally by an errant flower. Single canvas, 32 threads to 5 cm, is suitable. The vertical and horizontal stitches cover 4 threads. The diagonal border stitches cover 2 by 2 threads, except for the outside edge where they cover 3 by 3 threads.

Flower heads against zigzag stripes

A companion to the previous pattern, shown in figure 44 is one of tent stitch flowers in three shades of the same colour are against a background of irregular diagonal lines. This produces

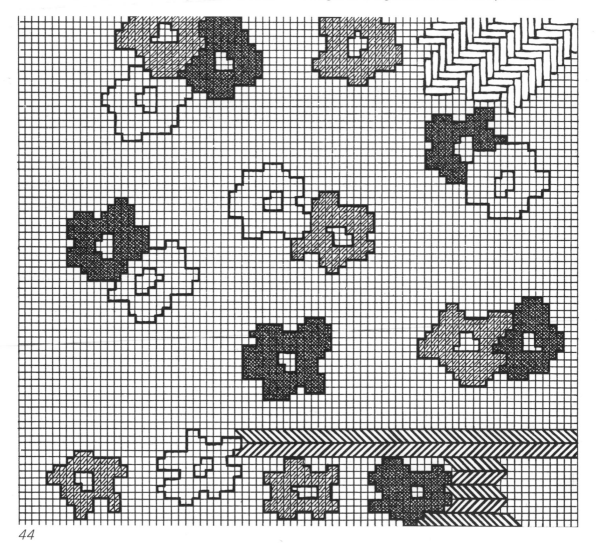

44

a slightly waffled texture in the embroidery which can look attractive. See figure 45. Here the flowers are stitched first. Each flower is worked in 2 shades only, for example, light and medium, or medium and dark, thereby giving the pattern more movement in light and shade than if all three shades were used for all flowers. The centres can be stitched in silk or stranded cotton. The diagram (see figure 45) indicates a general half drop repeat in the arrangement of the flowers, but they need not be repeated exactly. Two shades of a paler colour are used for the background. It is worked in

vertical straight stitches over 3 threads moving up or down 1 thread each time to give a diagonal line. Light and medium shades are used in alternate lines to give a slightly striped effect. These diagonal lines change direction at irregular intervals as they criss-cross around the flowers. Provided the diagonals remain true, this background can be worked freely without repetition, the diagram serving only as an indication. Single canvas of 32 threads to 5 cm is most suitable, though the pattern can be worked on double canvas, 20 threads to 5 cm. In this case the background should be done in tent stitch

45

46a   *Japanese flower*

instead of straight stitches. The flowered border against diagonals, shown in figures 27a and 27b, makes a good frame around this design. By reversing the flower and background colours for the border, a more interesting balance of light and dark can be produced.

Japanese flower

This is another pattern combining tent stitch flowers with a straight stitch background. See figures 46a and 46b. Diagonal lines criss-cross to form diamond shapes that contain a stylized

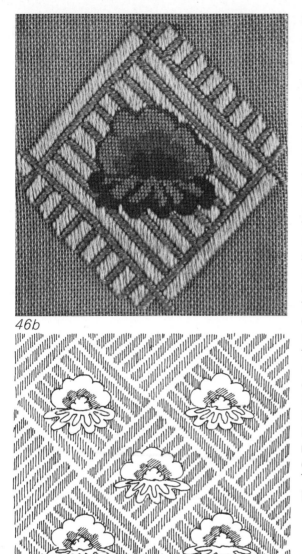

46b

46c

flower against a diagonally striped ground. The direction of the diagonal filling alternates from diamond to diamond. Flowers may be worked in every diamond or every alternate row of diamonds. Three shades are needed for each flower, but the colours can vary from flower to flower. The lattice pattern is worked first. Horizontal stitches over 3 threads make up the diagonal lines which meet from opposite directions at stitches 1 and 34. As the left line crosses the right, an extra stitch over 1 thread is required first on the left side, and on the next row up on the right side. It is important to check that the corresponding corners of the diamond are in line. The top of the tent stitch flower is placed on the sixteenth row down from the top corner of the diamond. The stripes are filled in after the flower has been worked. Two shades are used, the lighter for vertical stitches covering 6 threads, and the darker for horizontal stitches over 3 threads. This is not the easiest design to work because of the accuracy required for marking out the lattice pattern. Single canvas, 32 threads to 5 cm, is suitable. This pattern can be repeated to form long narrow shapes as well as squares.

Lettering

Letters make beautiful patterns. As well as containing a message they are interesting and decorative shapes. See figure 47. For church embroidery, especially kneelers, letters on their own can provide a complete design, possibly just spelling the name of the church. Initials combined with flowers or border patterns can decorate cushions, bags or purses. Words made up of letters of different styles can often happily be put together, as seen on posters or tombstones. Letters of different sizes may also be used together. Good letters are not easy to draw, particularly when they have to be adapted to fit the rigidity of threads in canvas. Most of the less elaborate types of lettering can, however, be adapted to canvas embroidery. With a little patience and accurate measuring the letters can be transferred to graph paper, provided the scale is not too small to destroy the subtlety of the shape.

It is essential to plan the word on paper first. The most effective way of spacing embroidered letters is to allow each letter to sit in the same amount of space, measured approximately in terms of general area. This cannot be done by counting squares between the end of one letter and the beginning of the next: compare the closeness of A to J, with that of M to N. Draw out each letter to be used on graph paper. Then transfer them one by one to tracing paper shifting it to and fro until the spacing is felt to be right in relation to the last letter. The spacing can then be measured in terms of squares by placing the tracing paper over the graph paper again. Two alphabets are offered here with suggestions for various ways of interpreting them. The letters O and I have been omitted as Q and H respectively give the necessary information.

Sans serif

This is a simple letter face (see figures 48a and 48b) that can be treated in various ways. The shape of each letter may be emphasized by an outline in a darker or lighter colour. This makes the letters appear less heavy.

A pattern that is unrelated to the shape of the letter can be used as decoration, for example, a diagonal stripe, as shown in figure 48a. A different version of this is the use of plain letters against a striped background. Another effective way of decorating the letter is to divide it into facets, working these in strongly contrasted tones to suggest a three-dimensional effect. On the basis that the light is striking each

48a   Sans serif

49a   Egyptian

letter from the same angle, it is possible to draw up the tonal values consistently, even on curved letters. The letters S and K show how a shadow on one side and underneath can give the letter thickness. See figure 48b. Worked on single canvas, 32 threads to 5 cm, the letters measure 3 cm high. On double canvas they measure 5 cm, being 20 threads high.

Egyptian
As this style of letter is slightly more elaborate than the last (see figures 49a and 49b), only one version of it is described. It may be worked in tent stitch on various meshes of canvas, or in encroaching gobelin stitch on single canvas, 32 threads to 5 cm. The centre of the letters are worked in the darkest colour shading through medium to light at top and bottom. These letters are 1 thread taller than the sans serif described immediately above.

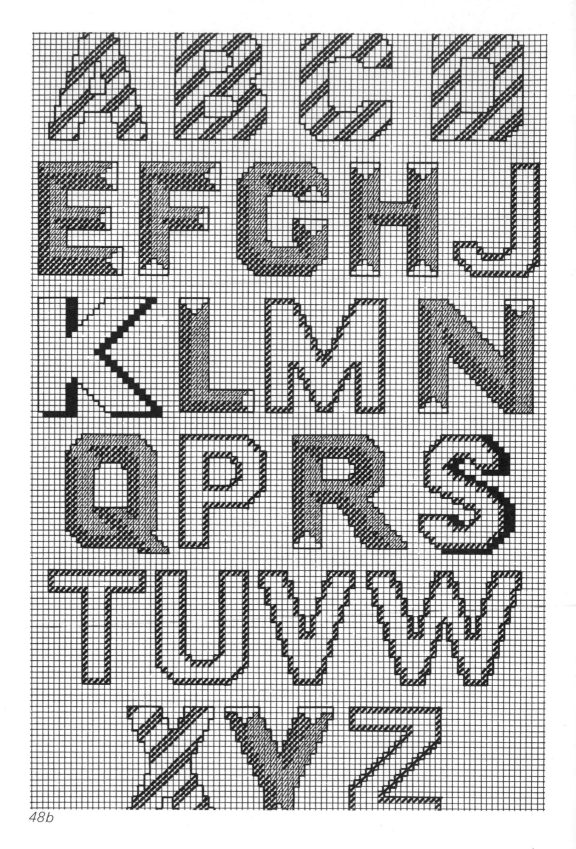

48b

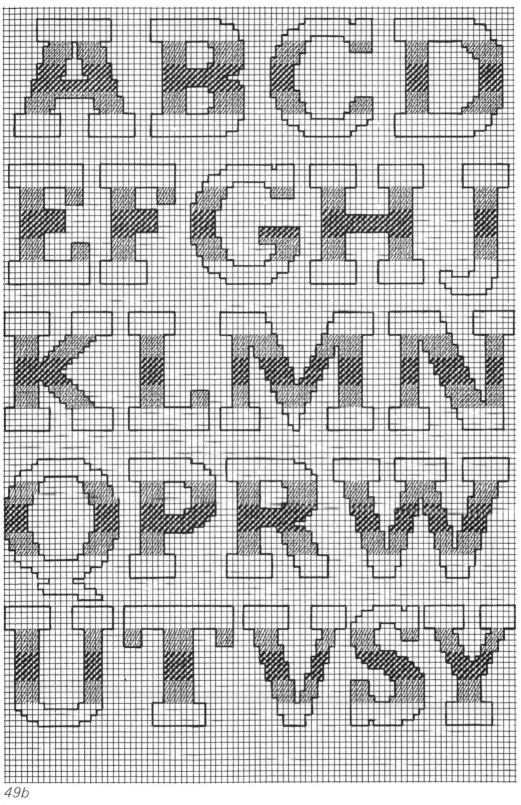

49b

Stitches that make patterns

Though all stitches have a certain pattern value by virtue of being repeated, some of the more elaborate ones have sufficient shape to make interesting patterns as they are. Inevitably, colour can enrich such patterns, though often a simple grading of shades repeated at intervals is enough. Sometimes the pattern is formed by the contrast of one stitch shape with another, thereby creating a textural pattern. Each of two contrasted stitch patterns might be developed separately, yet harmoniously joined together to give a contrapuntal pattern. The slanting ladders pattern shown in figures 55a and 55b is an example of this. Many more patterns could be developed along these lines.

Wheatsheaves

The stitch motif worked in a half drop repeat automatically makes a pattern with a hard nubbly texture. See figures 50a and 50b. The motif is made up of 5 vertical straight stitches in a row covering 6 threads. These are bound together half way down with 2 short horizontal stitches which cover 2 threads of the canvas at the back. See the diagram in figure 50b. The half drop is formed by the next wheatsheaf starting in line with the binding stitches. The first and last of

50a   Wheatsheaf

50b

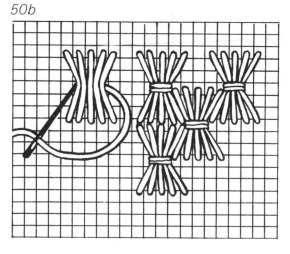

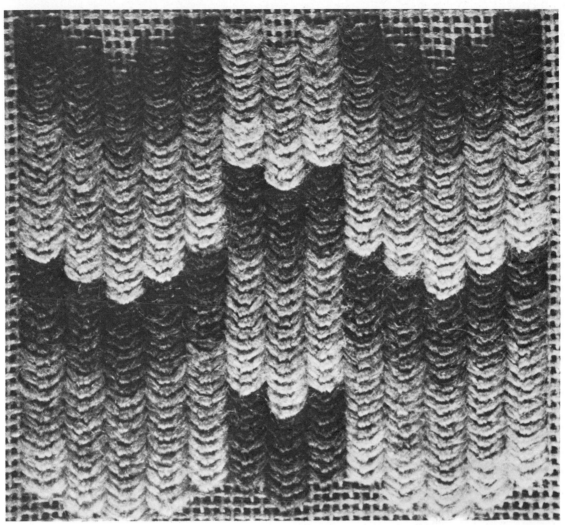

51a   Organ pipes   51b

the 5 vertical stitches are worked in the
same hole as the binding stitches of the
sheaves on either side. Shaded effects
can be produced by working each
successive horizontal row of sheaves in
a darker colour. See figure 50a. This
stitch can also be used combined with
other stitches. Regularly placed against
a background of tent or gobelin stitch,
the wheatsheaves stand up in relief. It is
a fairly quick stitch to work on single
canvas of 28 or 32 threads to 5 cm, and
gives a firm, thick surface.

Organ pipes

Fly stitch worked in 5 shades of one colour make up this pattern. By grouping the lines into scalloped shapes an effect of organ pipes can be produced, as shown in figures 51a and 51b. Though the rows run vertically, they are best worked across. For example, in a group 5 rows wide, 4 stitches of the darkest colour are worked going down the first row; in the next row the first stitch starts 2 threads lower; in the third row, 2 threads lower again, in the fourth 2 threads up, and in the fifth, 2 threads up again, back in line with the first row. This same pattern is worked in all the shades in their respective order, beginning again with the darkest. By staggering the position of the shades in the next group of 3 rows, the pattern is further enriched, while the next group of 5 rows is like the first. Keeping the shading as described, a larger piece of work could also range from warm to cool colours, giving a rich rainbow effect. This stitch is only suitable for canvas of 32 or 36 threads to 5 cm. It requires practice to stitch evenly, but gives a close, fairly hard-wearing surface.

Leaves

Leaf stitch is used throughout this pattern. See figures 52a and 52b. In an all-over repeat, it is quite quick to work on single canvas 32 threads to 5 cm. By using 4 shades of 1 colour an extra richness is achieved. The shading fills a cone shape starting at the top with one leaf of the lightest shade, 2 leaves of the next lightest, 3 leaves of darker and then 4 leaves of the darkest at the bottom. In every alternate row of cone shapes, the shading is inverted with the lightest leaf at the bottom and the 4 darkest making a row at the top. This arrangement gives a kind of chevron stripe effect. The pattern looks well with the continuous leaf border pattern, shown in more detail in figures 31a and 31b.

52a   Leaves

Marbling

This is a good background pattern for covering a large area. The shapes are reminiscent of patterns on marbled paper. See figures 53a and 53b. Straight stitches worked horizontally over 4 threads are stepped to make a scallop pattern. Each scallop consists of 6 stitches. In a line going up, the second stitch is forward 2 threads from the first, the next is forward 1 thread, forward again 1 thread and 3 stitches in line, then back 1 thread, then back 2 threads in line with the first stitch, and the pattern repeats again. Occasional irregularities in the working of this basic scallop will set the pattern out of line and asymmetrical areas between the scalloped lines will appear. These are filled with tent stitch, which, like the scallops, can be worked in several shades of one or more closely related colours. Where the tent stitch covers a large area, spots made up of straight stitches are worked first to break up the flatness. This pattern is used around the arch in the basket of flowers design shown in plate 2. It could also serve as the central area of a cushion, perhaps with a wide border of flowers, on canvas 32 threads to 5 cm.

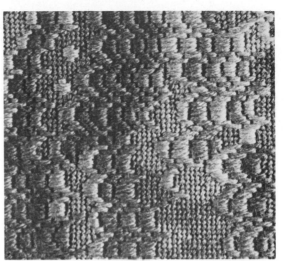

53a   Marbling

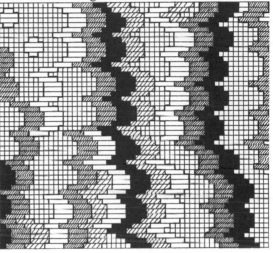

53b

Patches of turf

This design has a strongly textured effect similar to a sculptured carpet. An irregular arrangement of parallelograms of cut velvet stitch are set against a darker background of tent stitch. See figures 54a and 54b. The parallelograms vary slightly in size and proportion. At the sides and corners they may be trimmed down to triangles in order to fit the available space. The colouring of the background is broken up by using several similar shades worked to give a streaky effect. The areas of velvet stitch

52b

65

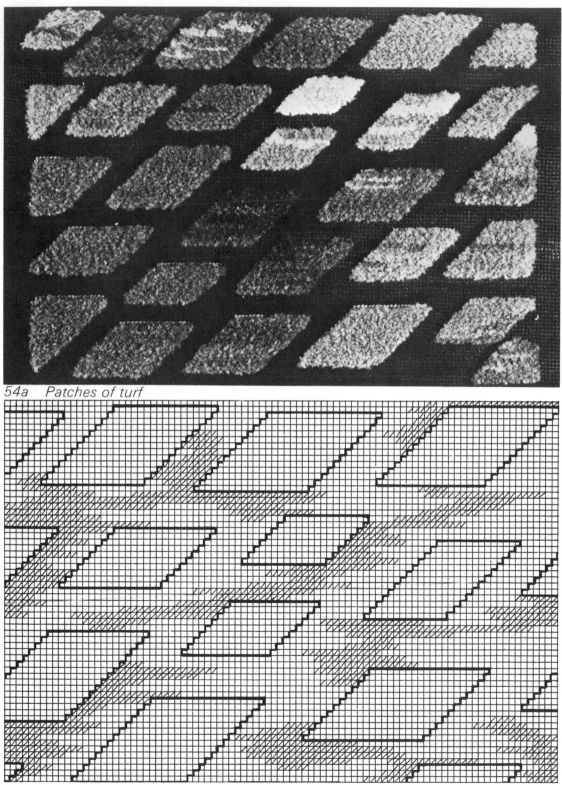

54a   *Patches of turf*

54b

66

also vary in colour, subtly within each patch. They range from pale green to maize colour from one patch to another. Because the velvet stitch has a pile, it appears to occupy a greater area of canvas than in fact it does. The horizontal lines between the patches are about 7 to 10 stitches high, and the diagonal lines 9 to 12 stitches wide. Areas of velvet stitch would also look well arranged in trefoils or leaf shapes. Though slow to work and rather extravagant on wool, velvet stitch is hard-wearing, and looks very rich. When choosing the colours, err on the pale side as velvet stitch appears shades darker when cut. This design is shown in colour.

Slanting ladders

This large scale pattern, shown in figures 55a and 55b, is suitable for a big cushion or duffle bag. The ladders are set on the true diagonal, each one 36 threads wide. The rung effect is achieved by padding with 2 strands of rug wool. Each vertical stitch goes over 4 threads of canvas as well as the padding. The stitches leave a small gap at each end of the step because the diagonal cuts into the shape. The fringed ends of the rug wool cover this gap. *Readi-cut* rug wool is convenient to use. The ladders are worked in 3 shades though the padding is all of the same colour. The background is also shaded, but not necessarily to coincide with the ladders. It is worked in brick stitch over 4 threads, and 5 shades are used. Because brick stitch is an interlocking stitch the colours can be shaded into each other gradually. The diagram (see figure 55b) only gives an indication of the area covered by each shade, no allowance being made for the rows where the colours are mixed. The width of these stripes of background shading can be

55a   *Slanting ladders*

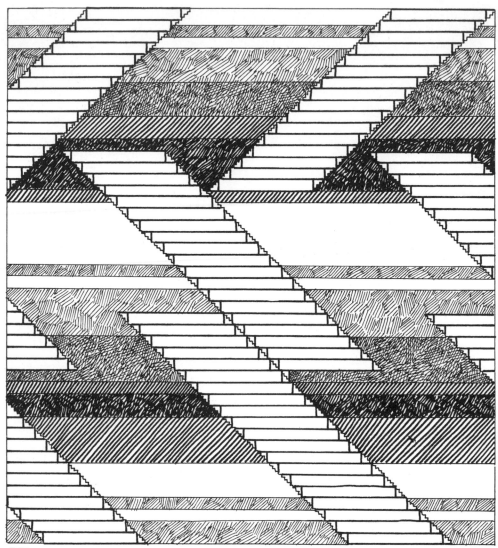

55b

measured against the ladders where each rung represents 4 threads.

The ladders are set 70 threads apart at the top and bottom of the diagram. The lowest ladders are not given their full length in the diagram: working from the base upwards, there are 18 rungs of the lightest colour, 9 rungs of the medium colour, and 5 rungs of the darkest colour. The centre ladders have 12 rungs of the lightest colour, and 7 rungs of the medium colour. The top ladders have 5 rungs of the lightest colour, 5 rungs of the medium colour, and 6 rungs of the darkest colour.

The easiest way to work this design is to mark out with tacking thread the diagonal spaces for the ladders, and then to work the brick stitch background. The padded stitches are then filled in, and the edges of the rug wool trimmed. Single canvas, 36 threads to 5 cm, gives the best cover, though 32 threads is probably adequate. This method of stitching over rug wool can be adopted as a method of securing handles or fastenings.

Stitches

Methods of working certain stitches vary. What to one generation may be an acceptable way of working a stitch, may give less satisfaction to the next. Not only do the methods gain or lose in popularity, but certain stitches themselves become fashionable or neglected. The following are a selection of the most widely used stitches, but this is by no means a complete list, and there are always new variations to try out. Sometimes a stitch may be known by several names. The names given here are those in fairly general use. The term 'backing' means the thickness of wool on the wrong side of the work. A strong or thick backing makes for harder wear, though inevitably it is more extravagant with wool. Many stitches can be worked to give almost the same effect on the right side, but with considerable difference in the weight of the backing. Usually, the thicker backing is the better one. The kind of canvas used also affects the way the stitch is worked, double canvas having different requirements from single.

Tent stitches

This is one of the most useful stitches, because its fineness gives maximum flexibility to the designer. It is made by crossing the intersection of one horizontal and one vertical thread of canvas. The direction of this diagonal stitch should be top right to bottom left. There are two basic methods of working the stitch on single canvas. Provided the wool is right for the canvas the scale of mesh can vary from fine to coarse.

Continental stitch
Worked this way the stitch is longer on the back than it is on the front. The direction of stitching is similar to a back stitch worked in horizontal rows. See figure 56. There is, however, a tendency for the canvas to be pulled out of shape, but this can be rectified with stretching. It is not recommended to work tent stitch in horizontal rows with a short vertical stitch on the wrong side. The backing is altogether too thin.

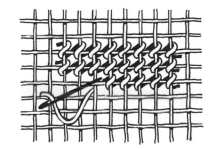

56   *Continental stitch*

Basket weave stitch
With this method the canvas keeps its shape. For large areas of background, etc., it is the most suitable method. The direction of the stitches moves upwards diagonally and downwards diagonally. See figure 57. The stitches on the wrong side alternate between horizontal on the up diagonal, and vertical on the down diagonal. When worked evenly the right side looks very smooth, and the wrong side has the appearance of neat darning. It is also a hard-wearing stitch.

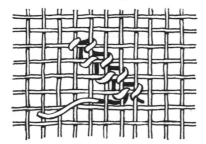

57   Basket weave stitch

Tent stitch with tramé threads
On double canvas either of the last two methods may be used if the wool is thick enough. If not, tramé lines can be laid down. These are horizontal stitches of wool which may be up to 5 cm in length, and are laid between the double threads. See figure 58. The continental version of tent stitch is then used to cover them. When working the tramé stitches, it is important that the joins in

58   Tent stitch with tramé threads

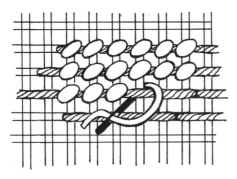

the stitches do not coincide vertically on each horizontal line of double threads, otherwise gaps in the stitches might be visible after the continental stitch has been worked.

Cross stitch

This is a harder-wearing stitch than the last one, and can be worked with the same thickness of wool to canvas. The vital factor is keeping all the crosses going in the same direction. See figure 59. It may be done by crossing each tent stitch one by one, or by working a horizontal row of continental stitch, and then travelling back along the line to cross the stitches. It is adequate to use a short stitch on the back when crossing continental stitch. With this method the canvas keeps its shape, and the temptation to cross in the wrong direction is virtually eliminated.

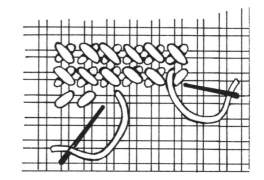

59   Cross stitch

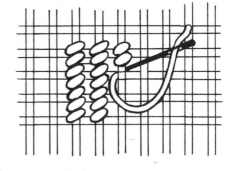

60   Rep stitch

Rep stitch

This is another stitch that covers double canvas closely, and gives a fine, hard-wearing surface. Each stitch splits the double threads horizontally while covering both vertical threads. See figure 60. There should be a long stitch at the back, as with continental stitch, and the rows are worked vertically. Interesting geometric patterns can be tried in this stitch as it lends itself to arrangements of sharply acute angles.

Gobelin stitches

Gobelin stitches form a group of several variations. Basically, they resemble the effect of true tapestry, hence their name, so called after one of the great French tapestry workshops. They are best used on single canvas.

Straight gobelin stitch
This usually covers 2 or 3 threads of canvas and is worked in horizontal rows. By using a thread of wool as padding, a richer texture can be achieved, and the chance of the canvas showing through is eliminated. See figure 61.

Encroaching gobelin stitch
This stitch is useful as it covers the canvas more effectively without padding. It is worked at a slight angle, not a true diagonal, across 1 thread and up 2 threads, or possibly across 2 and up 3 or 4 threads. See figure 62. By interlocking the next horizontal row into the last, a very close cover is produced. The interlocking of stitches further softens the merging of colour if a shaded effect is required.

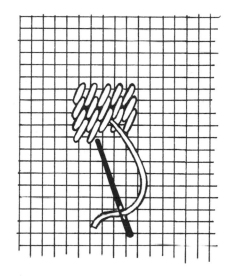

62   Encroaching gobelin stitch

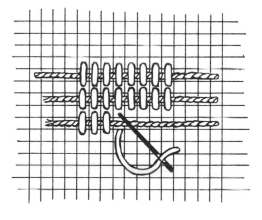

61   Straight gobelin stitch

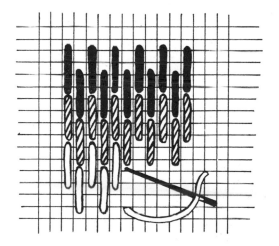

63   Brick stitch

Brick stitch
This is also one of the gobelin group, and again lends itself well to shaded effects. See figure 63. It may cover 4 or 6 threads of canvas, every alternate stitch being a half drop. It may be worked in a zigzag movement or horizontal rows. It is a fairly hard-wearing stitch.

Knitting stitch

As its name suggests, this stitch has the appearance of fine stocking stitch. See figure 64. It can be worked on double or single canvas. On the latter it produces a hard-wearing surface. Each stitch travels across 1 thread and up 2, with a short stitch at the back. It is worked in vertical rows up or down, the direction of the slant alternating in each row.

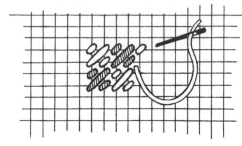

65   *Mosaic stitch*

Scotch stitch

The version shown here, in figure 66, is one of several variations of this stitch. It is in fact an enlarged development of mosaic stitch. Each square of 5 by 5 threads is covered by diagonal stitches worked from one corner to the opposite corner. The direction of the diagonal alternates from square to square. This gives a dark and light check effect even when worked in the same colour. It is fairly easy to design geometric patterns with this stitch, see the mirror frame, in colour. On single canvas of 32 or 36 threads to 5 cm, Scotch stitch produces a fairly hard-wearing surface.

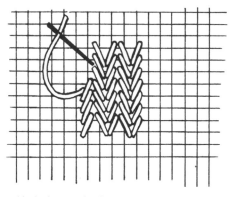

64   *Knitting stitch*

Mosaic stitch

A good background filler or stitch for geometric patterns, mosaic stitch is fairly hard-wearing on fine canvas, say 32 threads to 5 cm. It is not suitable for double canvas. It consists of little blocks, each of 3 diagonal stitches, over 1 by 1, 2 by 2, and 1 by 1 threads. These little blocks may be worked in horizontal or diagonal rows. See figure 65. Checkerboard or diagonal stripe patterns suggest themselves in this stitch.

66   *Scotch stitch*

Byzantine stitch

An extension of Scotch stitch, Byzantine stitch gives a strong diagonal step pattern. It is more effective worked in alternate rows of 2 shades. See figure 67. It is only suitable for single canvas and when worked fine is fairly hard-wearing. The length of stitch may vary, as also the number of stitches in each step. The diagram here shows diagonal stitches over 2 by 2 threads. There are 5 stitches in the vertical row, and 5 on the horizontal. Keeping this number accurate is vital to the pattern. In other versions the stitch may cover 3, 4 or 5 inter-sections of threads, and the step may be 4, 6 or 7 stitches in length. Byzantine stitch is a useful background filler, giving interesting effects with slight changes of colour. It is used in the petrol stains pattern shown in figures 16a and 16b.

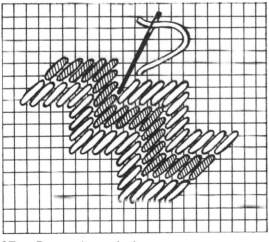

67　Byzantine stitch

Knotted stitch

This is similar to an encroaching gobelin stitch except that it has a short stitch tying it down. It can be used on double or single canvas. See figure 68. The longer stitch travels across 1 thread but up 3 threads. It is then crossed by a diagonal short stitch at the centre. Each successive row of stitching encroaches one thread into the row before, thus meeting the lower end of the tying down stitch of the row before. This is a hard-wearing stitch when worked fine, but not an easy one to manipulate into irregular shapes.

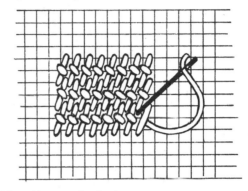

68　Knotted stitch

Fly stitch

This is a stitch that can be worked over different counts of canvas thread. Only single canvas is suitable. The stitch can travel over 4, 6 or even 8 threads, and the centre stitch can be spaced further down to give a sharper angle. The centre stitch always covers 1 thread. The diagram here illustrates a stitch covering 4 threads with the centre stitch placed down 1 thread and over 1 thread. See figure 69. Worked fine on canvas of 32 threads to 5 cm, it is a fairly hard-wearing stitch. It will work up success-fully into stripe or block patterns, but will not fit irregular shapes easily.

69　Fly stitch

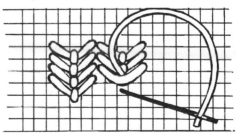

70 Web stitch

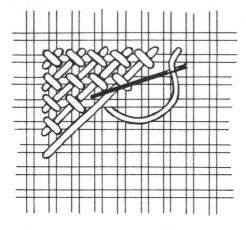

covers quite quickly but is not the hardest wearing of stitches.

Web stitch

Using tapestry wool, web stitch fits double canvas 20 threads to 5 cm, or single canvas 28 or 24 threads to 5 cm. The stitch is worked diagonally with a long thread laid first on the true diagonal. It is tied down with small stitches which cross it at right angles from every hole in the canvas, running the length of the long thread. On the second row the small stitches occur in between those of the first row. See figure 70. This stitch can be used to fill a square or rectangle, or it can be used for long diagonal lines. It is important that the true diagonal is always observed, otherwise the long stitch appears crooked. It is a fairly hard-wearing stitch, and resembles a darning pattern.

Herring-bone stitch

This is easier to work on double canvas or single canvas not finer than 28 threads to 5 cm. It is worked in horizontal rows over 2 by 2 double threads. To keep the threads overlapping in the right order, each row must start from the same side. See figure 71. It is not an easy stitch to fit into awkward shapes and is best kept for blocks or stripes. It

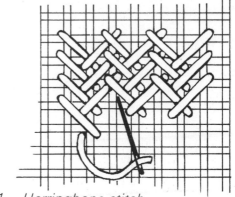

71 Herringbone stitch

72 Leaf stitch

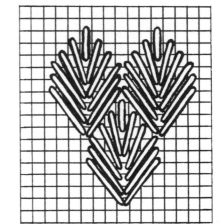

Leaf stitch

As its name implies, this stitch gives an all-over pattern of leaf shapes. Each leaf consists of 5 stitches working up towards the centre stitch, and then 5 stitches down the other side. See figure 72. Working from the centre, the first 3 stitches travel up 4 threads, and across 3. The fourth stitch travels up 4 threads but across 2, and the fifth stitch up 4 and across 1 thread. The centre stitch covers 3 threads, the top being 1 thread higher than the fifth stitch. The other side is similar but in reverse. In a horizontal row, each leaf meets the next one in the same holes of the canvas. The next horizontal row of leaves fits between the leaves of the last row, the first stitch emerging from the same hole as the third and ninth stitches of the last row of leaves. Single canvas of 32 or 28 threads to 5 cm is the most suitable. With the latter a centre stitch as a main vein can be added. This is not a very hard-wearing stitch.

French knot

A single twist of wool around the needle gives a neat knot when pulled tight. The needle needs to cross one intersection of canvas threads before returning into the canvas otherwise the knot might be pulled right through to the back. See figure 73. To get a close knot, it is a help to hold the end of the wool with the left hand while pulling the needle through the twist. French knots can be used for centres of flowers, etc. They make the blackberries on the raffia bag in colour plate 4. They are hard-wearing but slow to work.

appear complicated to work, it is only a cross stitch with an extra loop between the two stitches. Like tiling a roof, it must be worked horizontally starting at the bottom row. See figure 74. A short diagonal stitch is worked first over 1 intersection of canvas threads. Another stitch is worked over this and left hanging in a loop, and then a final tent stitch in the opposite direction holds down these two stitches. To ensure an even length of loop, the stitches may be worked over a knitting needle. The loops may be cut or left uncut. With tapestry wool, velvet stitch fits double canvas of 20 threads to 5 cm. It is also suitable for a coarser canvas with thicker wool.

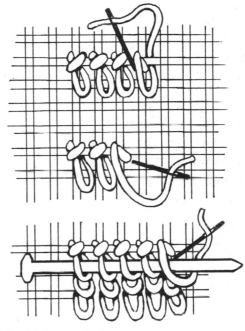

74   Velvet stitch

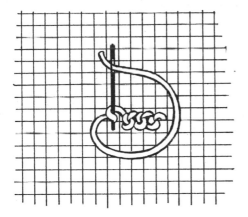

73   French knot

Velvet stitch

Though slow to work, this is a very rich textured stitch that wears well. It can be used alongside smoother stitches to accentuate its thickness. Though it may

Binding stitch

This is a very useful stitch for finishing
a hem, or for joining two pieces of canvas together. It can be used for double
or single canvas. A hem of unworked
canvas of approximately 1 cm should be
folded back one thread beyond the last
row of embroidery. In the case of single
canvas allow two threads to form the
fold. The binding stitch is then worked
along this ridge of canvas, single or
double thickness for hem or seam
respectively. See figure 75. The first 2
stitches are like little overcasting
stitches, and then the needle travels
back over 2 threads of canvas to the
beginning. From here the stitch is like a
herring-bone, forward over 3 threads
and back over 2 threads. It produces a
neat finish like a plaited effect. When
used for a hem, the lining can be
brought close to the stitching on the
inside edge, and hemmed neatly with
sewing thread.

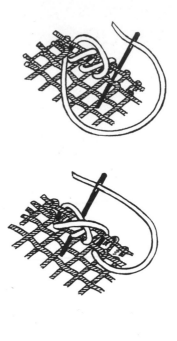

75   *Binding stitch*

Stretching

After the embroidery has been worked
the canvas will need to be pulled back
to its original shape. Some stitches pull
the canvas out of shape more than
others, but all work will benefit from a
little stretching. Damp the work with
cold water and pull the canvas in the
opposite direction from the way it has
been drawn up during stitching. See
figure 76a. If necessary snip into the
selvedge edge. Worked in tent stitch, a
square shape may become distorted to a
diamond shape and the canvas will
need pulling against the grain of the
stitching all over. Compare the length of
the diagonal measurements to discover
whether the shape is true. A T-square is
also a help in checking that the horizontal lines of stitching are true to the
vertical ones.

Once the original shape has been
retrieved, pin the work to a board with
drawing pins. See figure 76b. Working
from the centre of one side pull firmly to
the centre of the opposite side and pin,
extending the pinning outwards to the
corners. Stretch the other two opposite
sides in the same way. Leave pinned to
the board until quite dry. The more
distorted the piece of work the more
damping it requires.

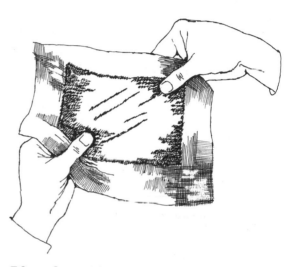

76a   Stretching

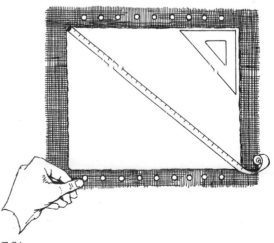

76b

Finishing

It seems a pity that so much good work should be ruined by poor finishing. Often the reason for this is simply lack of planning in the early stages, and a failure to match the construction and shape of the piece to the embroidered design. If the end product has been thought out and the method of making up fully understood the results will be far more rewarding and successful. Years ago when there was a much narrower choice of ready-made frames, fittings and edgings, the needlewoman had to rely on her own ingenuity and craftsmanship in putting the work together. The making up should be just a further extension of the embroidery using, if possible, the same materials and methods.

Joining canvas

Seam join
Where an invisible join is required, as at the corners of a one piece kneeler, or in a long gusset, leave a gap in the embroidery for 1 cm on either side of the seam. Back stitch the two pieces, right sides together, making sure the threads of the canvas coincide. Embroider over the join, keeping the turnings free. Where a tramé thread is used, this should travel over the seam and will

help to give a completely continuous line of stitching. See figure 77a.

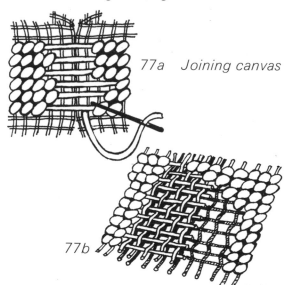

77a *Joining canvas*

77b

Overlap join
This method of piecing together is suitable for rugs where several people may be engaged on the same work, or where the size of work exceeds the width of canvas available. Again leave a gap in the embroidery on either side of the seam. Lap the edge of one piece of canvas over the other and tack firmly in place matching the threads of the canvas exactly. Trim the turnings so that the area of double thickness is 2 to 4 cm wide, depending on the mesh of the

canvas. Embroider over the double thickness as though it were single. This makes a very firm join. See figure 77b.

Seaming canvas to other fabrics

The combination of canvas with other fabrics is used mostly for cushions or bags. Fabrics that combine well with canvas embroidery are those of approximately the same weight and thickness. Examples are: soft leather, suede, velvet, corduroy, firm wool rep, or any woollen cloth of coat weight. To make a canvas-work cushion with a plain fabric back, back-stitch the canvas and fabric, right sides together, if anything slightly easing the fabric to the canvas. See figure 78. Work with the canvas side facing you, and stitch into the holes of the last row of embroidery. Allow a gap of 15 to 20 cm to pull through to the right side. It is possible to make a neat seam without the threads of canvas showing even without a fringe or piping. Before pulling through to the right side trim the turnings of canvas. At the corners, cut off a triangle of turning and draw the adjacent turnings together with over-casting stitches. See figure 78b.

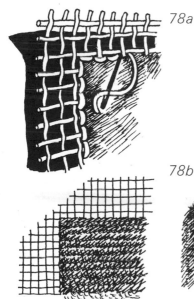

78a   Backstitch seaming, for seaming canvas to other fabrics

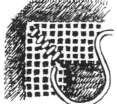

78b   Corners

Applying canvas to another fabric

If a large enough area of embroidery is used the canvas may be inset into the material using a backstitched seam. This may or may not need a braid hand-stitched over the seam.

If the strip of embroidery is narrow, it should be appliqued on to the back-ground fabric. See figure 79. Fold back the turnings at the last line of embroidery and hem neatly into the holes of the canvas, catching it down to the fabric with a matching thread. If velvet or other thick fabric is used, the canvas will sink happily into the pile.

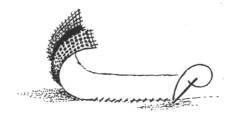

79   Appliqué canvas, for applying canvas to another fabric

Seaming canvas to canvas

When making up a bag or other article, it is often difficult to join the two pieces of canvas together without the threads showing. There are many decorative ways around this problem.

Binding stitch
This is a simple method of stitching two pieces together or turning in a hem. It is best worked along the straight of the grain, and gives a neat herring-bone pattern.

Overcasting
This can be done successfully along a curved edge, particularly if a thread of rug wool is used as padding. This extra fullness prevents the canvas showing. See figure 80a. Sometimes it is better to stitch into the second row of embroidery

rather than the first. This corded edge is suitable for a hem or a seam.

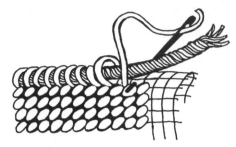

80a Overcasting, for seaming canvas to canvas

Piping
This gives a good finish to a seam. The cord is first encased in a strip of bias cut fabric. This is then tacked firmly to one piece of the canvas. The other piece is tacked to it right sides together and the seam is then back stitched. See figure 80b.

Silk cord
A silk cord can also be used to decorate a seam. It is easier to do than the piped seam which requires practice. The seam is first back stitched from the inside. The silk cord is then caught down along the seam with small stitches working from the right side. Alternatively, a handmade cord in 2 colours of wool can be used. On the flap of a bag, the cord can be left free to form a loop for a button.

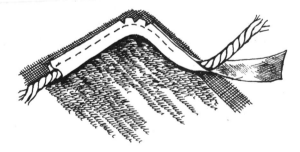

80b Piping for seaming canvas to canvas

Leather trim

For belts and bags particularly, leather gives a very professional looking finish. The stitching holes must first be marked in the leather strip which is placed right up against the last row of embroidery stitches. See figure 81. A running stitch or saddle stitch is suitable, so that the leather trim looks the same from both sides. This method produces a neat edging over a hem, or joins two pieces together, either canvas to canvas, or canvas to leather. Leather can also be used as a backing or lining to a canvas work bag, belt or shoes. Rubber solution is the best adhesive, as it retains its flexibility when dry.

Fringes

A double row of velvet stitch makes a thick fringing. Wrapping the loops around a thick knitting needle gives enough length to the fringe which may be cut or left uncut.

Lengths of cut wool can be hooked into the canvas with the ends pulled through the loop to give a knotted fringe. See figure 82a.

Where a longer fringe is required, say at the base of a decorated bag or head cushion, longer threads can be hooked and knotted into the canvas to make a more elaborate fringe. These may then be gathered into groups using needle weaving (see figure 82b), wrapping, or macramé techniques.

Tassels

These can be made by wrapping wool around a piece of thick card. See figure 83a. Tied together at the top and cut through at the bottom, the tassel may be bound round at the centre with wool or silk (see figure 83b). Crewel wool makes the finest tassels, and the colour might be darker at the centre than at the outside.

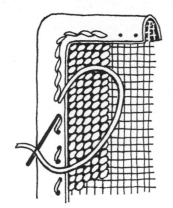

81　Leather trim

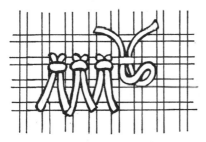

82a　Knotted fringe
82b　Needleweaving for fringes

83a　Tassels

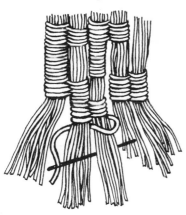

83b

Handmade cord

Two threads of wool, possibly of contrasted colours, are knotted together at one end and pinned to a board. A loop is knotted in one thread to start off. Using alternately one thread and then the other, loops are formed and pulled through each other continuously, similar to finger knitting. It is important to keep the tension even. See figure 84.

84　Handmade cord

Buttons

Glass or wooden beads with large holes can make good fastenings. Bring the kneedle up in the position the button is needed, thread the bead on to it, and then wrap the thread around the bead going through the hole about four times. Stitch back into the fabric leaving a long enough stitch for a shank. Continue this process until the button is completely covered with threads. Finish by wrapping the shank firmly with several twists of thread and end off. A silk thread could be used for this. See figure 85. A button covered in the same fabric as the lining material does well for a bag or belt fastening.

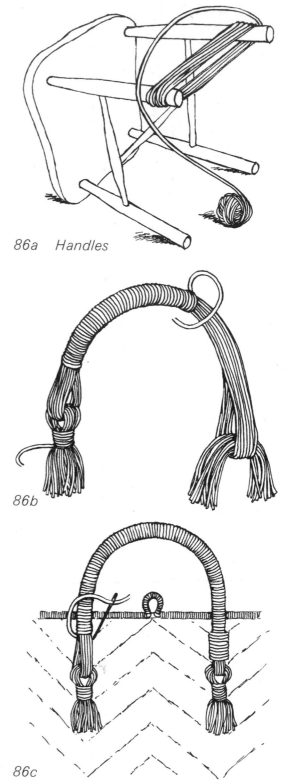

86a   Handles

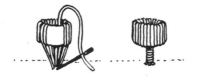

85   Buttons

Handles

It is important that these should be well constructed as they always seem to show signs of wear first. On small bags they could be a continuation of the corded finish. On larger bags they might be made by the same method on a thicker scale. Determine the length of handle needed. Space two pegs apart at the required distance, or chair legs might do. See figure 86a. Wind the wool around the legs enough times to give sufficient thickness. Keeping this wool in position, wrap more wool tightly around it until a firm cord is produced. See figure 86b. Leave enough uncovered length at each end to attach the cord with stitching to the canvas. The stitching should continue the effect of the wrapping. See figure 86c. If a small loop is left outstanding at the end of the handle a thick tassel could be threaded through. Where handles travel right

86b

86c

82

around the girth of the bag they can be made in one continuous cord.

Attaching ready-made frames

Sometimes ready-made frames and handles are fitted with small holes by which to attach them to the fabric. The stitching can be worked through these to make a pattern. The lining should be stitched into the bag before the frame is attached. To hide the wrong side of the stitching on the inside of the bag a narrow ribbon ruched with a gathering thread can be stitched just inside the frame. See figure 87. There is usually enough rebate in the frame to allow for this extra thickness.

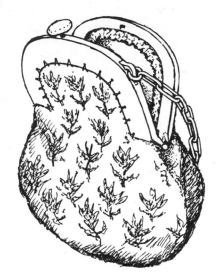

87   Attaching ready made frames

Linings

Bags, belts, etc., made of canvas embroidery do need to be lined. The work deserves a good fabric, silk or good quality substitute, or possibly a printed cotton with a small pattern. For bags, the lining should be made up fractionally smaller, and hemmed neatly into the corded or binding-stitched edge. If a leather trim is used, the lining should be attached to the canvas work first, and the turnings trimmed together.

Things to make

Here are some suggestions for items to make, and ways of constructing them. In almost every case it is worth making a paper pattern first.

Upholstery

Here the shape is governed by the piece of furniture itself. Even so, it is possible to devise patterns that relate to it. To outline the area to be embroidered, a large piece of brown paper is pinned to the upholstered part of the chair, stool, etc., and the shape is marked out on it. Allow the embroidery to extend marginally into the turnings to ensure complete cover. Re-upholstering the finished embroidery is best done by a professional.

Kneelers

These are easily constructed. There are two basic methods. Either the sides and top can be worked from the same piece of canvas; see figure 88, or the top can be worked separately from the gusset, which is seamed to it after stretching. These two methods of construction also apply to stool tops with a deep stand of upholstery above the frame.

Bags

There are so many simple yet interesting kinds of shapes, handles and fastenings that it is unimaginative to suppose a ready-made bought frame to be the only

88   Kneelers

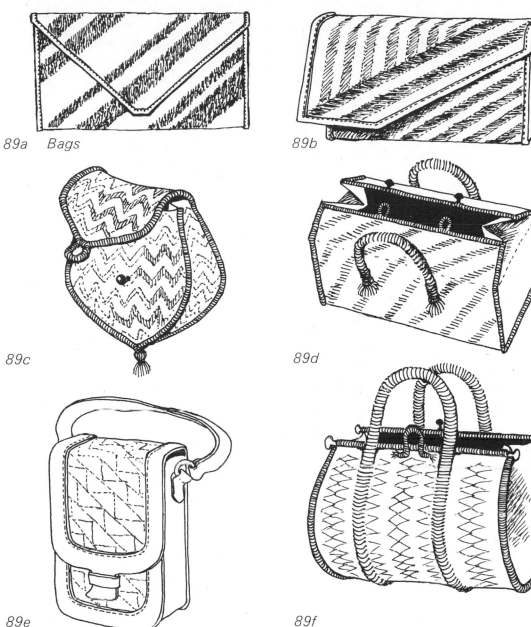

89a   Bags

89b

89c

89d

89e

89f

answer. Occasionally pretty frames are to be found, particularly second hand ones. The over-all shape of the bag should then be designed to fit the character of the frame, and the stitching selected to match the scale of its proportions. Most of the following shapes may be made in various sizes ranging from purses to work bags.

Envelope bag
One of the simplest and easiest shapes is that of an envelope with a right-angled point at the flap. It is easier to make if the point is slightly blunted. See figure 89a. It can be square or rectangular. Silk cord, leather binding, or over-casting over rug wool would make suitable finishes. An invisible fastening

or button with a loop of the corded edge can be used.

Clutch bags
These are a further development of the envelope bag, with perhaps a strap at the back. See figure 89b. The addition of leather gussets would make a more capacious shape.

89g

Shield-shape bag
This is a shield shape with a flap, made of 4 pieces, the 2 side pieces being narrower at the top than the front and back, and thus acting as gussets. See figure 89c. The edging can be of silk cord or wrapped rug wool, the ends of which can be worked into a tassel. A loop at the back can fasten the bag to a belt. The bag shown in figure 89c has a button and loop fastening.

Gladstone bag
Here the front, back and base are made of one continuous piece of fabric. See figure 89d. The side gussets are square in shape which give a box type bag. The front and back fold down over the top and fasten, possibly with toggles and loops. One handle can extend over the top, or two handles can be fitted on either side.

89h

Satchel bag
This is made with a gusset all round to which the strap is attached. See figure 89e. The flap is worked in one with the back and fastened with a strap and buckle. Leather seems the obvious choice of trim. It may require professional making up unless the embroideress is practised at leatherwork.

Work bag similar to a tool bag
One continuous piece of fabric makes this bag, with D shaped gussets at each side. See figure 89f. The handles can be worked into the embroidery round the

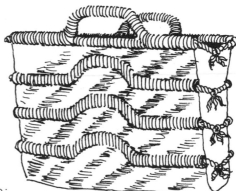

89i

girth of the bag to give more strength, thus dividing the shape into three sections. At the opening, the canvas can be bound over metal or wooden rods to give a firm edge. In another version of this work bag, the wrapping of the rug wool handles is continued over the rods, thus securing them in place. See figure 89i. The decoration on the rest of the bag can follow this shape. The ends of the rug wool used for the padding can be drawn together into tassels at the sides, revealing the gusset lining.

Work bag with wooden handles
Simple wooden handles with a cut-out slot can be used quite effectively. See figure 89g. The fabric of canvas work is seamed down one side and along the bottom edge. Allow approximately 15 cm or 6 in. of the fabric between the handles. This folds in to form a gusset when the bag is carried.

Duffle bag
A rectangle of canvas work is seamed to make a cylinder, which is then attached to a circular base of leather or strong fabric. See figure 89h. The top of the cylinder is finished with stitching over a padding of rug wool, from which loops are worked at intervals. A cord is threaded through these to make a handle. Loops threaded with tassels decorate the rest of the bag.

Cushions

These are the most popular things to make. Though they come in many sizes and shapes, their construction is comparatively easy to design. As they are usually backed with a plain fabric, the area of stitching to be covered need not be too formidable. Square cushions need to be at least 35 by 35 cm; rectangular cushions, 30 by 20 cm, the minimum for small head cushions of

this shape; round cushions need to be 30 cm in diameter, or more; as also do octagonal cushions. All the cushions described above can have gussets to make them squab cushions. See, as examples, figures 90e and 90f.

Less embroidery is needed where an embroidered inset is used to decorate a cushion; for example, a square cushion may have a narrow border of embroidery appliqued on to plain fabric (see figure 90a); or it may be constructed with a mitred frame of plain fabric around an embroidered centre (see figure 90b). A rectangular cushion may have a centre panel of embroidery inset with braid or fringed edging (see figure 90c); or a bolster shape may have an inset panel of embroidery, as in figure 90d. Here a continuous border pattern can be used to give a cylindrical design with inconspicuous join.

90a
Cushions

90b

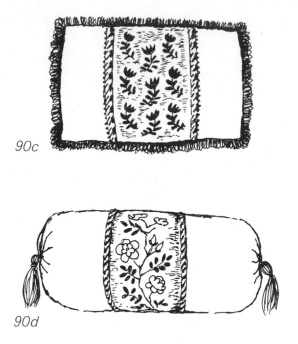

90c

90e

90d

90f

As with making up bags, the time and effort given to good finishing is always worth it. Some kind of decoration is usually necessary to conceal any canvas which might show through along the seams. Where possible make the fringe or tassels by hand, or work a double row of velvet stitch along the edge. A narrow piping cord covered in the plain fabric of the cushion back is suitable for use with a gusset.

Pelmets

The quality of firmness in the fabric combined with its decorative properties makes canvas-work a suitable choice for pelmets. A border of flowers, vines or geometric shapes would look rich hanging above plain curtains. Because of the height at which most pelmets are seen the scale of the work can be fairly coarse, otherwise the prospect of covering so great an area might seem rather daunting. The shape of the pelmet will not only be goverened by the window, but also by the pattern used. Some border patterns fit neatly into a scalloped

shape which could then be edged with fringing or tassels. See figure 91a. For a high window a *trompe-l'oeil* effect of swags can be worked, and then edged with real tassels. See figure 91b. On a much finer scale, narrow pelmets can be used to decorate shelves or over-mantles.

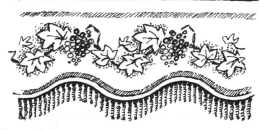

91a   Pelmets

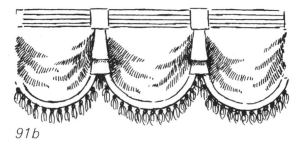

91b

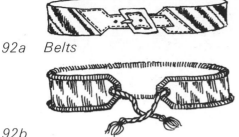

92a   Belts

92b

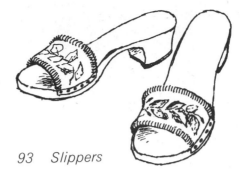

93   Slippers

Belts

Many of the border patterns described earlier would make suitable belts, or straps for bags. The maximum width that is comfortable to wear is probably 7.5 cm or 3 in.; and 2 cm is the minimum width needed to show the embroidery. Backed with leather, as shown in figure 92a, with a narrow leather binding and strap and buckle fastening, an embroidered belt looks tailored and smart. Finished with a corded edge worked over rug wool, and a hand-made cord or toggle type fastening, the effect is softer, as figure 92b demonstrates.

Slippers

Men's carpet slippers or women's mules make up well in canvas work. Patterns and scale of stitching need to be small, and the stitch a hard-wearing one. Little geometric patterns or small flowers, and sometimes initials are suitable. For mules, the simplest shape consists merely of a wide strap similar to a *Scholl* sandal. See figure 93. The mule in colour plate 4 was made in two pieces, seamed and edged by overcasting over rug wool. The uppers were lined with suede and tacked on to the wooden soles with coloured gimp pins. For the traditional shape of slipper, a better finish is obtained if the stretched embroidery is steamed into shape over a last or shoe-tree.

94   Spectacle case

Spectacle case

An envelope of 2 pieces approximately 8 cm wide by 15 cm long makes a simple case for spectacles. The canvas needs to be a fine one, and thin chamois would make a good lining. The 2 sides can be joined neatly with binding stitch which would also make a suitable finish at the open end. See figure 94.

Mirror or photograph frame

Decorative mounts for photographs or glass can be worked in various shapes, for example, octagons, squares, rectangles with lozenge-shaped cut-outs, etc. See figures 95a and 95b. The design of the embroidery needs to relate to the shape of the frame. Neat, repeating patterns or flowers can be used. A fine mesh of canvas is suitable, but the stitch need not be a hard-wearing one. When finished, the canvas is wrapped around a firm card backing with the turnings stuck down on the wrong side. A very narrow braid or thin leather strip will probably be required around the inside edge to prevent the canvas showing, particularly at the corners. The whole mount with glass or photograph can then be fixed into a wooden picture frame.

Rugs

Though slow to work, these can be both beautiful and practical. As canvas is sold in narrow widths, only a small rug can be made in one piece. The necessity of having to join the canvas can produce interesting designs, such as square or octagonal panels, medallion shapes, etc., possibly divided by narrow border patterns which conceal the joins. See figure 96. These joins must be made while the embroidery is being worked. See figure 77b. A hard-wearing stitch is essential for a rug, for example, tent stitch, cross stitch or velvet stitch. Canvas of 14 or 10 double threads to 5 cm is suitable.

95a   Mirror frame

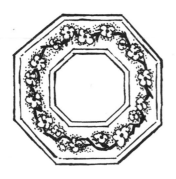

95b

96   Rug

90

Suppliers

Great Britain

Embroidery threads and accessories
Mrs Mary Allen
Turnditch, Derbyshire

Art Needlework Industries Limited
7 St Michael's Mansions
Ship Street
Oxford OX1 3DG

The Campden Needlecraft Centre
High Street
Chipping Campden
Gloucestershire

Craftsman's Mark Limited
Broadlands, Shortheath
Farnham, Surrey

Dryad (Reeves) Limited
Northgates
Leicester LE1 4QR

B Francis
4 Glenworth Street
London NW1

Fresew
97 The Paddocks
Stevenage
Herts SG2 9UQ

Louis Grossé Limited
36 Manchester Street
London W1 5PE

The Handworkers' Market
8 Fish Hill
Holt, Norfolk

Harrods Limited
London W1

Thomas Hunter Limited
56 Northumberland Street
Newcastle upon Tyne
NE1 7DS

Levencrafts
45 Church Square
Guisborough, Cleveland

Mace and Nairn
89 Crane Street
Salisbury, Wiltshire SP1 2PY

MacCulloch and Wallis Limited
25–26 Dering Street
London W1R 0BH

The Needlewoman Shop
146–148 Regent Street
London W1R 6BA

Christine Riley
53 Barclay Street
Stonehaven
Kincardineshire AB3 2AR

Royal School of Needlework
25 Princes Gate
Kensington SW7 1QE

The Silver Thimble
33 Gay Street
Bath

J Henry Smith Limited
Park Road, Calverton
Woodborough nr Nottingham

Elizabeth Tracy
45 High Street
Haslemere, Surrey

Mrs Joan L Trickett
110 Marsden Road
Burnley, Lancashire

Women's Home Industries
Pimlico Road
London SW1

United States

Appleton Brothers of London
West Main Road
Little Compton
Rhode Island 02837

American Crewel Studio
Box 553 Westfield
New Jersey 07091

American Thread Corporation
90 Park Avenue
New York

Bucky King Embroideries Unlimited
Box 124c, King Bros
3 Ranch, Buffalo Star Rkc
Sheriden, Wyoming 82801

The Golden Eye
Box 205
Chestnut Hill
Massachusetts 02167

Lily Mills
Shelby
North Carolina 28150

The Needle's Point Studio
7013 Duncraig Court
McLean, Virginia 22101

The Thread Shed
307 Freeport Road
Pittsburgh, Pennsylvania 15215

Yarn Bazaar
Yarncrafts Limited
3146 M Street
North West Washington DC

Index